I0147732

Red Eagle and the
Wars With the Creek
Indians of Alabama
1812-1814

Red Eagle's Leap

Red Eagle and the
Wars With the Creek
Indians of Alabama
1812–1814

George C. Eggleston

LEONAUR

Red Eagle and the Wars With the Creek Indians of Alabama 1812-1814
by George C. Eggleston

Leonaur is an imprint of Oakpast Ltd

Material original to this edition and presentation of the
text in this form copyright © 2011 Oakpast Ltd

ISBN: 978-0-85706-623-7 (hardcover)
ISBN: 978-0-85706-624-4 (softcover)

http://www.leonaur.com

Publisher's Notes

The views expressed in this book are not necessarily
those of the publisher.

Contents

Preface

A work of this kind necessarily makes no pretension to original-
ity in its materials; but while all that is here related is to be found in
books, there is no one book devoted exclusively to the history of the
Creek war or to the life of William Weatherford, the Red Eagle. The
materials here used have been gathered from many sources—some
of them from books which only incidentally mention the matters
here treated, touching them as a part of larger subjects, and many of
them from books which have been long out of print, and are therefore inaccessible to readers generally. The author has made frequent
acknowledgments, in his text, of his obligations to the writers from
whose works he has drawn information upon various subjects. By
way of further acknowledgment, and for the information of readers
who may be tempted to enlarge their reading in the interesting history of the South-west, he appends the following list of the principal
books that have been consulted in the preparation of this volume:

Parton's *Life of Andrew Jackson*
Eaton's *Life of Andrew Jackson*
Pickett's *History of Alabama*
Drake's *Book of the Indians*
McAfee's *History of the Late War in the Western Country*
Claiborne's *Notes on the War in the South*
Meek's *Romantic Passages in South-Western History*
Indian Affairs, American State Papers
Kendall's *Life of Jackson*
Waldo's *Life of Jackson*
Russell's *History of the Late War*
Brackenridge's *History of the Late War*

Chapter 1

Red Eagle

It is a long journey from the region round about the great lakes, where Tecumseh lived, to the shores of the Alabama and the Tombigbee rivers, even in these days of railroads and steamboats; and it was a much longer journey when Tecumseh was a terror to the border and an enemy whom the United States had good reason to fear. The distance between Tecumseh's home and that of Red Eagle is greater than that which separates Berlin from Paris or Vienna; and when Tecumseh lived there were no means of communication between the Indians of the North-west and those of the South, except by long, dangerous, and painful journeys on foot.

A man of smaller intellectual mould than Tecumseh would not have dreamed of the possibility of establishing relations with people so distant as the Creeks were from the tribes of the North-west. But Tecumseh had all the qualities of a man of genius, the chief of which are breadth and comprehensiveness of view and daring boldness of conception. The great northern chieftain did many deeds in his day by which he fairly won the reputation he had for the possession of genius, both as a soldier and as a statesman; but nothing in his history so certainly proves his title to rank among really great men as his boldness and brilliancy in planning the formation of a great confederacy of the tribes, which extended in a chain from the lakes on the north to the Gulf of Mexico on the south. He was wise enough to learn of his foes. He saw that their strength lay in their union; that it was by "joining all their camp-fires," as he phrased it, that they made themselves irresistible; and as he saw with consternation that the great tide of white men was steadily advancing westward, he understood, as few men of his race were capable of doing, that there was but one possible way for the red men to withstand the ever-encroaching stream. Separately the tribes were powerless, because separately they could be beaten one by one. Troops who were engaged in reducing an Illinois tribe during one month could be sent the next to oppose another tribe in Mississippi or Alabama. Thus the secret of the white men's success, Tecumseh saw, lay in two facts: first, that the whites were united, working together for a common purpose, and helping each other in turn; and, second, that the whites used the same troops over and over again to fight the separately acting tribes.

Seeing all this and understanding it, Tecumseh conceived his great plan—a plan equally great, whether we regard it as a stroke of statesmanship or a brilliant scheme of military combination. He determined, as he said, to build a dam against the stream. He undertook to form a confederacy of all the tribes from north to south, to teach them to act together, and to oppose the advance of the white men by uniting that power which they were wasting separately.

It was in execution of this plan that Tecumseh made that journey to the South in the year 1811 which, in combination with other causes to be mentioned in their place, induced the Creeks of Southern Alabama to abandon all that they had gained of civilization, and to plunge first into a war among themselves, and afterward into that struggle with the white men which destroyed their nation almost utterly.

In that war there was one man more conspicuous than any other—more relentless, more daring, more desperate in his refusal to give or to accept quarter, and at the same time more brilliant in attack and defence, abler in counsel, and having greater skill in the field than any of his fellow-chiefs—a man who fought Jackson, Claiborne, Flournoy, Floyd, and Coffee, whose troops, coming from different quarters of the country, surrounded him on every side and outnumbered him on every field; fighting them with credit to his own skill and daring, and with no little damage to these skilled enemies—a man of whom Jackson said, "He is fit to command armies."

This man was Red Eagle, or, in his native Muscogee tongue, Lamochattee.

To the white men with whom he lived a great part of his life, and to his enemies in war, he was better known as William Weatherford; and as the historical accounts of the war in which he won his renown were all written by white men, because Red Eagle could not write, his white name, Weatherford, is the one by which he is generally known in books. His fame was won as an Indian, however; it was the Indian warrior Red Eagle, not the half-breed planter Weatherford, who did the deeds which gave him a place in American history; and this neglect of his Indian name in all historical works which refer to him is an example of the sarcasm of destiny. It reminds one of the hero of whom Byron tells us, who, falling in battle covered with glory, lost his only chance for fame by the blunder of a printer, who misspelled his name in the gazette. We have preferred to call the great commander of the Creeks by his Indian name, Red Eagle, on the title-page of this book, but in writing of him it will be necessary frequently to use the name Weatherford instead.

The story of the Creek war naturally follows the life of Tecumseh, with which this series of Indian biographies was introduced; and indeed the one story is necessary to the complete telling of the other. It may be best told in the form of a life of Red Eagle, who commanded on one side, and whose genius for command alone made the war an affair worth writing about; but, unluckily for the biographer, the materials for a biography of Red Eagle, in the strict sense of the word, are meagre and difficult to get at.

I hinted at the chief cause of this meagreness and obscurity when I said, just now, that Red Eagle could not write. I always thought, in reading Caesar De Bello Gallico, that the Roman commander had a great advantage over the poor Gauls in his rather remarkable dexterity in the use of the pen. We do not know how good or how bad his handwriting was; but whether he wrote with perfect Spenserian precision or in a scrawl as illegible as Mr. Greeley's, Caesar knew how to tell his side of the story, and there was nobody to tell the other side. Perhaps the tale would read very differently if some clever Gaul had been able to write an account of the war in classic Latin for the school-boys of the nineteenth century to puzzle out with the aid of a dictionary. So Red Eagle, if he had known how to write, would probably have given us a view of the things done in the Creek war which we do not get from his enemies.

It is not merely in the military sense that the word enemies is here used, but in the literal one as well; for very nearly all the information we have about Red Eagle and his performances is drawn from the writings and the spoken testimony of men who hated him with a degree of violence of which one can scarcely conceive in our time. These men wrote while boiling with the passions of a war which seriously threatened the existence of this American nation, and they hated Red Eagle as one of the men who added very greatly to the country's peril, and sorely taxed its resources when its resources were fewest. Their hatred was so violent that they could not restrain its expression; while they granted to Red Eagle the possession of courage and ability, they could not write of him without flying into a passion and heaping hard names upon his head.

One of them, in a grave treatise about the war, scolded in this way about him:

> Among the first who entered into the views of the British commissioners was the since celebrated Weatherford, with whom it may not be amiss to make the reader better acquainted at this time. Weatherford was born in the Creek nation. His father was an itinerant peddler, sordid, treacherous, and revengeful; his mother a full-blooded savage of the tribe of the Seminoles. He partook of the bad qualities of both his parents, and engrafted on the stock he inherited from others many that were peculiarly his own. With avarice, treachery, and a thirst for blood, he combines lust, gluttony, and a devotion to every species of criminal carousal.

That, certainly, is as pretty a bit of angry vituperation as one hears from the lips of the worst of scolds, and so wholly did the distinguished author of the book from which it is taken lose his temper, that he lost his discretion with it, and forgot that so coarse and brutal a fellow as he here declares Red Eagle to have been—a man so wholly given over to debauchery—is sure to show in his face, his person, and his intellectual operations the effects of his character, impulses, and habits. In the very next paragraph this writer tells us certain things about Red Eagle which forbid us to believe that he was a drunkard, a debased creature, a glutton, or a brute. He says:

Fortune in her freaks sometimes gives to the most profligate an elevation of mind which she denies to men whose propensities are the most virtuous. On Weatherford she bestowed genius, eloquence, and courage. The first of these qualities enabled him to conceive great designs, the last to execute them; while eloquence, bold, impressive, and figurative, furnished him with a passport to the favour of his countrymen and followers. Silent and reserved, unless when excited by some great occasion, and superior to the weakness of rendering himself cheap by the frequency of his addresses, he delivered his opinions but seldom in council; but when he did so he was listened to with delight and approbation.

That does not read like an account of the parliamentary methods of a brutish man, degraded by vice and debauched with drunkenness and gluttony; it sounds rather like a description of the wise ways of some Webster or Clay. Drunken men with the gift of eloquent speech do not hoard it and use it in this adroit way. This is not all, however. Men who are given over to vice, gluttony, and drunkenness usually carry the marks of their excesses in their appearance and their ways of thinking; but our writer who has told us that Weatherford was such a man, tells us how he looked and acted, and what his ability was, in this wise:

His judgment and eloquence had secured the respect of the old; his vices made him the idol of the young and the unprincipled. It is even doubted whether a civilized society could behold this monster without interest. In his person tall, straight, and well-proportioned; his eye black, lively, and penetrating, and indicative of courage and enterprise; his nose prominent, thin, and elegant in its formation; while all the features of his face, harmoniously arranged, speak an active and disciplined mind." A little further down the page this writer calls Weatherford "the key and corner-stone of the Creek confederacy," and characterizes him as "this extraordinary man.

Our purpose is not now to defend Red Eagle's memory or to extol his character, though there is good reason to remember him with honour for his courage in war and for his good faith in peace; and there are abundant proofs that the praise which the hostile writer whom we have quoted could not deny to the fallen chieftain, was far juster than the abuse he heaped upon him. We have made these extracts merely to show in what spirit of unfair prejudice all the contemporaneous accounts of Weatherford's life and deeds were written. It will be better to form our own opinions of the Creek warrior's character after we shall have reviewed the events of his life; and no one who so examines the facts, although they come to us only from his enemies, can fail to form a much higher opinion of the unfortunate man than that which the chroniclers of his day have offered to us ready-made.

The enmity and prejudice of which we have spoken operate still more strongly in another way to embarrass the biographer who seeks to learn details of Weatherford's life. Where the writers of his day have misrepresented his character or conduct, it is not difficult to discover the fact and to correct the misjudgement; but, unluckily, they too often neglected even to misrepresent him. Caring only for their own side and their own heroes, these historians, who were generally participants in the events they chronicled, took the utmost pains to tell us just where each body of American troops fought; who commanded them in the first, second, third, and so on to the tenth degree of subordinate rank; how many Americans and how many friendly Indians there were in each part of every field; how many of these were killed and wounded—everything, in short, which they could find out or guess out about the details of their side of the fight, while the other side seemed to them unworthy of any thing more than the most general attention. They were so careless indeed of the Indian side of these affairs that it is in many cases impossible to discover from any of the accounts what chiefs commanded the Creek forces in important battles, or even what chiefs were present. In other cases this information is given to us by accident, as it were, not in the accounts of the battles, but by means of a casual reference in an account of something else. Thus one of the writers devotes many pages and a good deal of stilted rhetoric to his account of the Fort Mims massacre, a bloody affair, in which Weatherford won solely by reason of the fact that he was a better and more skilful officer than the American commander, manifesting indeed some of the best qualities of an able general;

but with all this historian's minuteness of detail, he wholly forgets to mention the fact that Weatherford had anything to do with the matter. His neglect is not the result of any want of information, as is shown by the fact that, in writing of other things afterward, he incidentally mentions the Creek warrior as the leader of the Indians at Fort Mims.

To the carelessness of the contemporaneous writers, to whom alone we can at this day look for information upon detailed points of interest, must be added, as a cause of the meagreness of the record, their lack of opportunity. The Indians kept their own secrets. They were fighting to destroy the whites, not to win renown; and the Americans who fought them had little chance to hear news of any kind from the forces on the other side.

Notwithstanding this lack of detailed information respecting Red Eagle's life and deeds, however, we know with certainty that he was, as the writer quoted a few pages back said, the "key and corner-stone of the Creek confederacy," the commander of the Creek armies, the statesman who guided the Creek councils, and the general who planned and conducted the Creek campaigns. His was the master mind on the Indian side, as positively as Jackson's was on the side of the Americans; and therefore while there is an unfortunate lack of information of a strictly biographical nature concerning this remarkable man, it is still possible to write his life by writing an account of the Creek war. After all, it is the things a man does which make up his life; and the story of his deeds is his biography, whether or not it includes the dates of his birth and his death, or tells with precision when or how he did this or that.

Accordingly, instead of beginning this story of Red Eagle's life with a chapter about his birth and parentage, after the customary manner of grave biographers, and following his career incident by incident, confining the narrative to an account of his direct, personal share in each transaction, I shall write an account of the war he made, regarding the whole series of events as properly parts of one great affair which Red Eagle devised and executed.

To make such an account clearly intelligible, however, it will be necessary first to recount briefly the history of the Southern Indians, and to show who and what the Creeks were, what their condition was at the time of the war's beginning, and what they hoped to gain by their contest with the whites—which was not by any means a mere outbreak of savagery like some of the Indian troubles of our time, but rather a war deliberately undertaken with very definite purposes, after long consideration and no little getting ready.

Upon many points the best authorities are conflicting, partly because their works were written each with a special purpose and from a special point of view, and partly because of carelessness in the collection and weighing of facts; but it is still possible to arrive at the truth in all essential particulars, and to construct, out of the fragmentary materials at command, a consecutive account of the brilliant campaign of 1813-14, in which Red Eagle was the foremost figure on one side, and Andrew Jackson the master spirit on the other.

CHAPTER 2

Red Eagle's People

Red Eagle, or William Weatherford, was only in part an Indian, as we shall see presently; but his life was so entirely the life of an Indian, in that part of it at least which gave him his title to a place in history, that we must naturally think of him as a member of his mother's race, rather than as a white man, and we must regard the Indian nation to which he belonged as his people. He was born a Creek, and not only so, but a great chief of the Creek nation; that is to say, a chief of the highest hereditary rank.

The Creek nation was not a tribe, but a confederacy of tribes, united as the Roman Empire was by successive conquests. The original Romans in this case were the Muscogees, a tribe of Indians so much further advanced toward civilization when white men first encountered them than most of the Indian tribes were, that they had been able to preserve greatly more of their own history than savages are ordinarily able to do. They had fixed laws, too, not merely rules of the chase, but laws by which they were governed in the ordinary affairs of life; and many of their practices when the tribe was first known to white men indicate that they were then rapidly working out a system of government and semi-civilization for themselves, or else that, as they themselves believed, they were descended from a race formerly civilized, of whose civilization they still retained traces in their customs.

About the year 1775, an adventurous young Frenchman named Le Clerc Milfort visited the Creeks, and marrying a woman of the nation became a chief among them. After living with them for twenty years, he returned to France and was made a brigadier-general. In the year 1802, Milfort published a book about the strange people among whom he had lived half a lifetime, and from him, or rather through him, the world has learned what the Creeks believe to be the history of their nation.

This history, Milfort says, existed in the shape of a sort of record—not a written record, of course, but not merely oral tradition. The Creek historians had certain strings of beads, shells, and pearls which aided them somewhat as written books aid civilized men to preserve the memory of their nation's past. These beads meant different things according to their arrangement, and by their aid the historians were able to remember and transmit the traditions committed to their charge with something like accuracy.

The story, as they tell it, is probably apocryphal in most of its details, but it is less improbable, at worst, than is the story of the foundation and early history of Rome. According to the Creek historians, the Muscogees fought with the Aztecs against Cortez, and when the Spanish invader gained a secure foothold in Mexico they took up their march northward. On their way they encountered the Alabamas, whom they drove before them for years, following them from one part of the land to another, and giving them no rest. They chased the Alabamas to the Missouri River, thence to the Ohio, and thence to Alabama, whither they followed their steps. Finally, in the early part of the eighteenth century, the persecuted Alabamas despaired of finding a secure refuge from their relentless persecutors, and to save themselves from further destruction consented to form a close alliance with the Muscogees, submitting to the laws of their conquerors and becoming in effect Muscogees. This was the beginning of that confederacy which afterward became the Creek Nation. The Tookabatcha tribe, fleeing from their enemies in the north, sought the protection of the Muscogees next and became members of the nation. Other tribes were added to the nation one after another, until the confederacy, whose seat was in the region along the Alabama, Coosa, and Tombigbee rivers, became an empire, embracing in its rule all the people round about them, and carrying terror even to the tribes beyond the Savannah River.

The country which the Muscogee confederacy inhabited was and still is singularly well watered and fertile. Their two great rivers, the Alabama and the Tombigbee, are fed by numberless creeks of large and small size, and the number of these streams prompted the white men who traded with the Muscogees to call their land the Creek country, and from the land the name was transferred to its people, who were thereafter called the Creeks.

These Creeks, as we have said, had a sort of semi-civilization of their own when the whites first visited them. They had fixed rules and customs governing marriage and divorce. They lived in houses, wore scanty but real clothing, and were governed by a rude system of laws. Curiously enough, they even had a system of social caste among them, a sort of graduated order of nobility. There were certain families who held high hereditary rank, hereditary privileges, and hereditary authority—the family of the Wind, the family of the Bear, the family of the Deer, etc.; and of these the family of the Wind was the highest in rank and authority. They constituted, indeed, a sort of royal family, the family of the Bear ranking just below them.

When Colonel Benjamin Hawkins was sent on an important mission to the Creeks in the year 1798 he found an organized and somewhat complicated system of government in existence among them. Each town had its separate local government, presided over by a Micco, who belonged always to one of the chief families. They had their public buildings and pleasure houses, their fixed rules for the conduct of public business, for the promotion of warriors, and for all the other things which need systematic regulation.

Beginning thus with a foundation of recognized customs upon which to build a civilization, the Creeks improved rapidly under the influence of the white men when they were brought into contact with them. They already cultivated the ground, and, according to their tradition, had always done so. From the white men they learned to trade, to carry on their commerce with regularity, and even to manufacture cloths and other needed articles. They lived generally in peace with the white men, and, when the war that destroyed all this good beginning came, these people had their horses and their houses, their farms, their hoes, and their looms. They were not yet civilized, but they were well advanced toward the acquisition of the arts of peace. They had too much hunting land, and the spontaneous or nearly spontaneous productions of their rich soil and genial climate made living somewhat too easy for their good; but in spite of these strong incentives to idleness, the Creeks were steadily improving. Many of them intermarried with the whites, and in part adopted white men's modes of living. Missionaries went among them, and even the traders were in an important sense missionaries. Many of the Creeks learned to read and write, a few were educated men, most of these being half-breeds, whose fathers sent them north to attend schools.

Their condition was made the more favourable for advancement by the good treatment they received at the hands of the United States Government. It is constantly said in our time that the government has never dealt justly or kept honest faith with the Indians, and this reproach is usually coupled with a reference to the wiser, better, and more humane methods of the British in Canada; but if one were disposed to argue the question, it might easily be shown that both the assertion of the uniform failure of the Americans to deal justly with Indians, and the implication that the English have as uniformly treated the savages well, are false. In the case of the Creeks, it appears to be certain that the American Government did all that could be done to elevate the savages, and was only thwarted in the attempt by the interference of British agents—red and white—who incited Red Eagle's people to undertake the war which resulted in the destruction of their prosperity and their ultimate removal from the land they inhabited.

Mr. Nathaniel Herbert Claiborne, a prominent citizen of Virginia, and a man specially well informed on the subject, in a work which was written immediately after the Creek war ended, wrote as follows on the subject of the government's treatment of the Creeks:

It has been demonstrated that the conduct of the United States to the Creek Indians was both just and honourable. Without any consideration save that which arises from the consciousness of doing a good act, the government of the United States had, for more than twenty years, endeavoured to reclaim them from a savage to a civilized state. By the exertions of government, bent only on augmenting the stock of human happiness, it was evident that the situation of the Creeks was greatly ameliorated. Many of them spoke and wrote our language. Pious men were sent, at the expense of government, to instruct them in the religion of Christ. The rising generation were instructed in numerous schools.... A sentiment of pity, a fit cement for lasting friendship, had taken possession of the American breast toward the Indians; and our citizens and government vied with each other in acts of benevolence and charity toward them. They were instructed in the fabrication of the implements of husbandry. The loom and the spinning-wheel were in full operation through the whole nation; while the art of house-building, so essential to the accommodation of man and his protection from the winds and waters of heaven, was rapidly approximating to perfection. If any of our citizens injured them a punishment was provided by law, and the temper of the nation, in unison with the temper of the government, rendered its infliction certain. And such was the progress of the Creeks in civilization, and the obligations they were under to the United States, that no one believed they could be cajoled into a confederacy against us.

One other point must not be overlooked, because, although its bearing upon the prospects of the Creeks may not be fully evident to readers who have given the subject no attention, it was really the most promising thing in their situation. The tribal relation among them was weakening. They were taking the first steps from communism, which is the soul of savage life, to that individualism which is the foundation of civilization. They were beginning to hold individual property, and thereby to become men, with interests and wills of their own, instead of mere members of a tribe. This was brought about in part by their trading with the whites and in part by their intermarriages. The traders who married Creek wives and lived in the nation were shrewd fellows, strongly inclined to look sharply after their own interests; and their half-breed children, who retained their rank as Creeks, many of them being chiefs of high degree, inherited their fathers' instincts and learned their fathers' ways. It would not have required many years of peace in these circumstances to have made of the Creeks a nation of civilized men. Until the seeds of hostility to the Americans were sown among them by the agents of the British and the Spanish, their advancement was steady, and the effort which the Americans were making to civilize them was the fairest and most hopeful experiment perhaps that has ever been made in that direction on this continent.

CHAPTER 3

Red Eagle's Birth and Boyhood

William Weatherford, the Red Eagle, was born in the Creek country, and born a chieftain. The exact date of his birth is not known, but as he was a man of about thirty or thirty-five years of age when the Creek war broke out in 1813, his birth must have occurred about the year 1780. He is commonly spoken of in books, and especially in books that were written while a feeling of intense antipathy to him continued to exist, as the son of a Scotch peddler, or the son of a Georgia peddler, the phrase carrying with it the suggestion that Red Eagle was a man of contemptible origin. This was not the case. His father was a Scotch peddler, certainly, who went to the Creek country from Georgia, but he was by no means the sort of person who is suggested to our minds by the word peddler. He was a trader of great shrewdness and fine intellectual ability, who managed his business so well that he became rich in spite of his strong taste for the expensive sport of horse-racing.

Besides this, men usually have two parents, and Red Eagle was not an exception to this rule. If he was the son of a Scotch peddler from Georgia, he was also the son of an Indian woman, who belonged to the dominant family of the Wind; that is to say, she was a princess, her rank among the Creeks corresponding as nearly as possible to that of a daughter of the royal house in a civilized monarchy.

Red Eagle's connection with persons of distinction did not end here. He was the nephew of the wife of Le Clerc Milfort, the Frenchman mentioned in a former chapter, who, after a twenty years' residence among the Creeks, returned to France and received a brigadier-general's commission at the hands of Napoleon. Red

Eagle was the nephew, through his mother, of Alexander McGillivray, a man of mixed Scotch, French, and Indian blood, who by dint of his very great ability as a soldier, a ruler of the Creeks, and a wily, unscrupulous diplomatist, made a prominent place for himself in history. He was commissioned as a colonel in the British service; later he became a commissary of subsistence in the Spanish army, with the rank and pay of colonel; and finally he received from Washington an appointment as brigadier-general, with full pay. He is described by Mr. A. J. Pickett, in his History of Alabama, as "a man of towering intellect and vast information, who ruled the Creek country for a quarter of a century." Another writer says that Alexander McGillivray "became the great chief or emperor, as he styled himself, of all the confederate Muscogee tribes;" and adds:

He was a man of the highest intellectual abilities, of considerable education, and of wonderful talents for intrigue and diplomacy. This he exhibited conspicuously through the period of the American Revolution, in baffling alike the schemes of our countrymen, both Whig and Tory, of the Spaniards in Florida, of the British at Mobile, and of the French at New Orleans, and by using them simultaneously for his own purposes of political and commercial aggrandizement. A more wily Talleyrand never trod the red war paths of the frontiers or quaffed the deceptive black drink at sham councils or with deluded agents and emissaries.

Reading these descriptions of the character and abilities of his uncle, knowing how shrewd a man his father was, and remembering that his mother was a member of that family of the Wind who had for generations managed to retain for themselves the foremost place in the councils and campaigns of their warlike race, we may fairly assume that Red Eagle came honestly by the genius for intrigue and for command which brought distinction to him during the Creek war. He may fairly be supposed to have inherited those qualities of mind which fitted him to be a leader in that fierce struggle, and as a leader to hold his own surprisingly well against greatly superior numbers of good troops, commanded by Andrew Jackson himself.

When Charles Weatherford, the Scotch trader from Georgia, married the sister of General Alexander McGillivray, or Emperor

Alexander McGillivray, as he preferred to be called, he acquired by that alliance a measure of influence among the Creeks which few men even of pure Muscogee blood could boast. This influence was strengthened as his shrewdness and the soundness of his judgment made themselves apparent in the councils of the nation. More especially he made himself dear to the hearts of the Creeks by his skill in managing their diplomatic relations with the Spanish authorities in Florida, and the American agents.

In all this, however, the wily Scotchman served himself while serving the nation, and he rapidly grew to be rich. He lived, literally as a prince, at his home on the eastern bank of the Alabama River, on the first high ground below the confluence of the Coosa and Tallapoosa rivers.

Here he built for himself a home, and, still retaining his interest in commerce, set up a trading house. His love of horse-racing has already been mentioned, and now that he was a man of wealth and consequence it was natural that he should indulge this taste to the full. He laid out a race-track near his trading house, and devoted a large share of his attention to the business of breeding fine horses. Even in thus indulging his passion for horse-racing, however, Charles Weatherford was shrewd enough to make the sport contribute to his prosperity in other ways than by means of profitable gambling. He so managed the races as to attract his neighbours, principally the Alabamas, to his place of business, and so secured to himself their trade, which would otherwise have gone to the traders on the opposite side of the river, in the village of Coosawda.

Here William Weatherford was born, the son of the wealthiest man in that part of the country, and by inheritance a chief of the ruling family of the nation. He had for tutors no less competent men than his two uncles, Alexander McGillivray, and the accomplished Frenchman Le Clerc Milfort. Young Weatherford evinced the best capacity for acquiring knowledge, but it was only such knowledge as he wanted to acquire. Caring nothing about reading and writing, he refused to learn to read and write, and no persuasions would overcome his obstinacy in this particular. He took pains, however, to acquire the utmost command of the English language, partly because it was useful to him as a means of communication with the Americans, and partly because he found that command of a civilized tongue gave him a greater force in speaking his native Creek language, and it was a part of his ambition to be distinguished for eloquence in council. He learned French, also, but less perfectly, and acquired enough of Spanish to speak it in ordinary conversation. He travelled, too, for improvement, making several journeys while yet a boy to Mobile and Pensacola, picking up as he went whatever information there was to acquire.

He thus became in an important sense an educated man. He could not read or write, it is true; but it is probable that Homer was equally ignorant, and not at all certain that Hannibal or Richard Coeur de Lion, great commanders as they were, were much better scholars.

The chief function of education is to train the mind, and the chief difference between the educated man and one who is not so is that the mind of the one has been trained into a state of high efficiency while that of the other has not. Reading and writing offer the shortest roads, the simplest means, to this end; but they are not the only ones, and if Red Eagle had little or no knowledge of letters, he had nevertheless an active intellect, trained under excellent masters to a high degree of efficiency, and hence was, in the true sense of the term, a man of education.

In his tastes and instincts this son of a Scotchman was altogether an Indian. He devoted himself earnestly to the work of acquiring the knowledge of woodcraft and the skill in the chase which his people held in highest esteem. He was a notable huntsman, a fine swimmer, a tireless walker. He was a master marksman, alike with the bow and with the rifle. He was passionately fond of all athletic sports, too, and by his skill in them he won the admiration—almost the worship—of all the youth of his nation. He was the fleetest of foot of all the young men who ran races in the Creek villages, and his fondness for the sports of his people was so great that he was never absent from any gathering of the young men for contests of strength, activity, or skill, however distant the place of meeting might be. He was their chief by right of his accomplishments, as well as by inheritance as the son of Sehoy the princess. Especially in the great Creek game of throwing the ball—a game which closely resembled a battle between hundreds of men on each side, and one in which success was achieved only by great personal daring and endurance added to skill, bones being broken frequently in the rude collisions of the opposing forces, and men being killed and trampled under foot not infrequently—the young Red Eagle was an enthusiastic and successful player.

While yet a little child, Red Eagle showed that he had inherited his father's love for horses, and his persistence in riding races, breaking unruly colts, and dashing madly over the roughest country on the back of some one of his father's untamed animals, gave him the finest skill and most consummate grace of a perfect horseman. An old Indian woman who knew the young chief in his youth, telling of his daring, his skill, and his grace as a horseman, said, "The squaws would quit hoeing corn, and smile and gaze upon him as he rode by the corn-patch."

All these things added to Red Eagle's popularity with the old and young of his nation, and the daring and enthusiasm which he showed in the sports of his people were exercised frequently in their service. In the wars of the Creeks with neighbouring nations, the Choctaws and the Chickasaws, and in their campaigns on the borders of Tennessee, Red Eagle distinguished himself for courage, tireless activity, and great skill in warfare, even before he had reached manhood, so that when his growth was fully gained he was already a man of the widest and most controlling influence among the Creeks, by reason both of his birth and of his achievements.

His popularity was enhanced doubtless by the beauty of his face and the comeliness of his person, for all the writers who have described Red Eagle, and all the men of that time who have given oral accounts of him, agree in telling us that he was a singularly handsome man, with brilliant eyes, well-cut features, shapely limbs, and imposing presence.

That nothing which could help him to influence and power might be lacking, Red Eagle was gifted with eloquence at once stirring and persuasive. His natural gift had been cultivated carefully, and, as we have seen in a former chapter, he adroitly hoarded his power in this respect, taking care not to weaken the force of his oratory by making it cheap and common. He would not speak at all upon light occasions. While others harangued, he sat silent, permitting decisions to be made without expressing any opinion whatever upon the matters in dispute. It was only when a great occasion aroused deep passions that Red Eagle spoke. Then his eloquence was overwhelming. He won his audience completely, and bent men easily to his will. He knew how to arouse their passions and to play upon them for his own purposes. Opposition gave way before the tide of his speech. His opponents in debate were won to his views or silenced by his overwhelming oratory; and he who was his people's commander in the field was no less certainly their master in the council on all occasions which were important enough to stir him to exertion. He had vices, certainly, but they were the vices of his time and country, and there is no sufficient evidence that he carried them to excess, while his retention of physical and intellectual vigour afford the strongest possible proof of the contrary.

CHAPTER 4

The Beginning of Trouble

We all know how trouble begins. Whether a big or a little quarrel is the thing about which we inquire, and whoever the parties to the dispute may be, the trouble may always be traced back to some small occurrences which led to larger ones, which in their turn provoked still greater, until finally the trouble came.

We have seen that there was peace and justice between the Americans and the Creek Nation, and that the Creeks had every reason in their own interest to continue living upon friendly terms with the whites. A good many of them fully understood this, too, and sought to persuade others of it; and it is probable that when the first troubles came the great majority of the Creeks earnestly wished to keep the peace, and to make use of the means of advancement offered to them by the American Government and people. Unluckily, they were the victims of bad advice, and the old story followed: one thing led to another.

It is not easy, in this case, to say precisely what the one thing was which led to another. That is to say, it is not easy to determine what was the first of the long chain of events which led the prosperous and improving Creeks into dissensions, and thence into the war out of which they came a broken and disheartened remnant of a once powerful nation; but tracing the matter as far back as it is necessary to carry the inquiry, we discover that a public road was one of the earliest causes of the trouble.

The Creeks were made masters of their own country by the Treaty of 1790, and their absolute title to their lands was respected by the United States Government, which defended them rigorously against encroachments upon their domain. That government, having become possessed of a wide tract of territory lying west of the Creek Nation, toward which the tide of emigration was rapidly turning, wished to provide a more direct and better road than any that existed, and with that end in view sought permission of the Creeks to run the new Federal Road, as it was called, by a direct route through the Creek territory. The principal chiefs, beginning to learn some of the natural laws that govern commerce, saw that the passage of a good road through the heart of the nation would necessarily benefit them, and make their commerce with the outer world easier and more profitable. Accordingly these chiefs gave the Creek Nation's consent, and the road was made. Over this the people quarrelled among themselves, dividing, as wiser people are apt to do, into two fiercely antagonistic parties. Those of them who objected to the thoroughfare were seriously alarmed by the great numbers of emigrants who were constantly passing through their country to the region beyond. They said that they would soon be walled up between white settlements on every side. The land on the Tombigbee River was already becoming peopled to such an extent that the hope, which many of the Creeks had secretly cherished, of driving the whites away from the banks of that river and recovering the territory to themselves must soon be abandoned, and they held, therefore, that in granting the right of way for the road the chiefs had betrayed the nation's interests.

There never yet was a quarrel which somebody did not find it to his interest to stimulate, and in this case the Spanish settlers, or squatters as they would have been called if they had lived thirty or forty years later, did all they could to increase the bitterness of the Creeks toward those chiefs who were disposed to be friendly with the Americans, and toward the Americans. These Spaniards still insisted that the territory in which they lived, and from which they were gradually driven away, belonged of right to Spain, and they saw with great jealousy the rapid peopling of that territory with Americans. The agents of the British, with whom the United States was on the point of going to war, added their voice to the quarrel, stimulating the Spanish and the Indians alike to hostility. It was very clearly seen by these agents that an Indian war, especially a war with the powerful Creeks, would greatly weaken this country for its contest with Great Britain. Emissaries of the British infested the Creek country, stirring up strife and sowing the seeds of future hostility among them. The Spanish in Florida, although our government was at peace with Spain, willingly became the agents for the British in this work, and secret messages were constantly sent through them promising arms, ammunition, and aid to the Creeks in the event of a war.

All these things gave great anxiety to Colonel Hawkins, the agent who had charge of the Creeks, but the trouble was not yet in a shape in which he could deal vigorously with it. He called a council, and did all that he could to convince the Indians of the government's kindly disposition. The friendly chiefs assured him of their constancy, and their assurance lulled his suspicions somewhat. He knew these chiefs to be sincere, but neither he nor they knew to what extent their influence with the nation had been weakened.

Then came Tecumseh, who, in the spring of the year 1811, arrived in the Creek country, accompanied by about thirty of his warriors. He came with a double mission: as the agent of the British he was charged with the duty of preparing the tribes of the South to join in the approaching war, as soon as a state of war should be declared; as Tecumseh he came to execute his own purpose, namely, the formation of a great offensive and defensive alliance between the tribes of the North and those of the South, against the American nation and people.

Tecumseh did not come as a stranger to the Creeks. The fame of his exploits in the North had reached them, and he was known to them even more favourably in another way. Nearly twenty-five years before, Tecumseh, then a young man, had dwelt among the Creeks for about two years, and the stories of his feats as a hunter had lived after him as a tradition. Hence when he came again in 1811 he was a sort of hero of romance to the younger Creek warriors, a great man of whose deeds they had heard stories during their childhood.

On his way to the South, Tecumseh tarried awhile with the Choctaws and the Chickasaws, trying to win them to his scheme, but without success. In Florida, he made easy converts of the warlike Seminoles; and returning thence he visited the Creeks, arriv-

TECUMSEH ENTERING THE COUNCIL

ing in October. While Colonel Hawkins was holding the Grand Council at Tookabatcha, of which we have spoken, and was trying to placate the Creeks, Tecumseh, followed by his warriors, dressed in their most impressive savage costumes, consisting of very little else than buffalo tails and other ornaments, marched into the meeting. Marching solemnly round and round the central square of the town, Tecumseh, when he had sufficiently impressed the lookers-on with a proper sense of his dignity, went through the most solemn ceremonies of friendship with his hosts. Greeting the chiefs in the most cordial fashion, he and his followers exchanged tobacco with them—a proceeding which attested their fellowship in the strongest possible way.

In the main the Creeks received Tecumseh cordially, returning his protestations of brotherhood in kind; but one chief, Captain Isaacs, whose fidelity to his obligations as a friend of the whites was proved afterward on the battle-field, rejected the overtures of the men from the North. He shook his head when asked to shake hands; he refused to exchange tobacco; and, with the frankness of a brave man convinced of his duty, he told Tecumseh to his face that he was a bad man, and added, "You are no greater than I am."

Tecumseh had come to the council for the purpose of using it for his own ends, but while Colonel Hawkins remained he made no effort to put his plan into execution. Colonel Hawkins could have thwarted him, in part at least, if the wily Indian had openly avowed the object of his visit; but Tecumseh was too shrewd to do that. Colonel Hawkins prolonged the council from day to day, but still Tecumseh kept silence. Each day he would say, "The sun has gone too far today; I will make my talk tomorrow." But the tomorrow of the promise did not come while Colonel Hawkins remained, and finally, worn out with the delay, that officer brought his conference with the chiefs to an end and departed.

Then Tecumseh opened his lips. Calling the people together, he made them a speech, setting forth his views and urging them upon the Creeks. He told them that the red men had made a fatal mistake in adopting the ways of the whites and becoming friendly with them. He exhorted them to return at once to their former state of savagery; to abandon the ploughs and looms and arms of the white men; to cast off the garments which the whites had taught them to wear; to return to the condition and customs of their ancestors, and to be ready at command to become the enemies of the whites. The work they were learning to do in the fields, he said, was unworthy of free red men. It degraded them, and made them mere slaves. He warned them that the whites would take the greater part of their country, cut down its forests and turn them into cornfields, build towns, and make the rivers muddy with the washings of their furrows, and then, when they were strong enough, would reduce the Indians to slavery like that of the negroes. There is every reason to believe that Tecumseh was convinced of the truth of all this. He was convinced, too, that the whites had no right to live on this continent. He told the Creeks, as he had told General Harrison, that the Great Spirit had given this land to the red men. He said the Great Spirit had provided the skins of beasts for the red men's clothing, and that these only should they wear. Then he came to the subject of the British alliance, telling the Creeks that the King of England was about to make a great war in behalf of his children the red men, for the purpose of driving all the Americans off the continent, and that he would heap favours upon all the Indians who should help him to do this.

A prophet who accompanied Tecumseh followed him with a speech, in which he reiterated what his chief had said, but gave it as a message from the Great Spirit; still further to encourage the war spirit among them, this teacher by authority promised a miracle in behalf of the Creeks. He assured them that if they should join in the war they would do so at no personal risk; that not one of them should be hurt by the enemy; that the Great Spirit would encircle them wherever they went with impassable mires, in which the Americans would be utterly destroyed, with no power or opportunity to harm the divinely protected Indians.

All this was well calculated to stir the already moody and discontented Creeks to a feeling of hostility, and when the speech-making was over there was a strong party, probably more than a majority of the Creeks, ready and anxious to make immediate war upon the Americans. Colonel Hawkins's long labours in the interest of peace had been rendered fruitless, and the war party in the nation was more numerous and more firmly resolved upon mischief than ever.

Tecumseh's labours were not yet finished, however. As a shrewd politician works and argues and pleads and persuades in private as well as in his public addresses, so Tecumseh, who was a particularly shrewd politician, went all through the nation winning converts to his cause. He won many, but although he was received as an honoured guest by the chief Tustinnuggee Thlucco, or the Big Warrior, he could make no impression upon that wise warrior's mind. It was not that Big Warrior was so firm a friend to the whites that nothing could arouse him to enmity. He had his grudges, and was by no means in love with things as they were; but he foresaw, as Tecumseh did not, that the war, if it should come, would bring destruction to his nation. He estimated the strength of his foes more accurately than his fellows did, and was convinced that there was no hope of success in the war which Tecumseh was trying to bring about. He was valorous enough, but he was also discreet, and he therefore obstinately remained true to his allegiance. His obstinacy at last roused Tecumseh's ire, and it was to him that Tecumseh made his celebrated threat that when he reached Detroit he would stamp his foot on the ground and shake down all the houses in Tookabatcha—a threat which it is said that an earthquake afterward led the Creeks to believe he had carried out. The story of the earthquake is repeated by all the writers on the subject, but some of the accounts of it contradict facts and set dates at defiance; and so, while it is not impossible and perhaps not improbable that an opportune earthquake did seem to make Tecumseh's threat good, the story must be received with some caution, as the different versions of it contradict each other. So, for that matter, it is not safe to trust the records upon any point, without diligent examination and comparison. Thus the fact that the battle of Tippecanoe was fought during this Southern journey of Tecumseh makes it certain that the mission was accomplished in the year 1811; yet Pickett, in his History of Alabama, gives 1812 as the year, and several other writers follow him. Again, some of the writers to whom we must look for the facts of this part of American history confound Tecumseh's two years' sojourn among the Creeks about the year 1787 with his visit in 1811, saying that that visit lasted two years—a statement which would make great confusion in the mind of any one familiar with the history of events in the North in which Tecumseh bore a part. A careful comparison of dates shows that Tecumseh started to the South in the spring of the year 1811, and returned to the North soon after the battle of Tippecanoe was fought— that is to say, near the end of the same year.

CHAPTER 5

The Civil War in the Creek Nation

We have called Tecumseh a wily politician, and in whatever he undertook his methods were always those of the political manager. He was quick to discover the temper of individuals as well as of bodies of men, and he was especially shrewd in selecting his agents to work with him and for him. He was not long in picking out Red Eagle as the man of all others likely to draw the Creeks into the scheme of hostility. Red Eagle's tastes and temper, as we have already seen, were those of the savage. He was a rich man, and had all the means necessary to the enjoyment of those sports and pastimes which he delighted in; but above all else he was an Indian. He looked upon the life of the white men with distaste, and saw with displeasure the tendency of his people, and more especially of his half-breed brothers, to adopt the civilization which he loathed. Moreover, he cherished a special hatred for the Americans—a hatred which his uncle and tutor, General McGillivray, had sedulously instilled into his mind in his boyhood; and this detestation of the Americans had been strengthened by the British and Spanish at Mobile and Pensacola, during his frequent visits to those posts. His favourite boast was that there was "no Yankee blood in his veins."

Besides his prejudice, Red Eagle's judgment taught him to fear the encroachments of the Americans, and men are always quick to hate those whom they fear. Red Eagle saw with genuine alarm that the white men were rapidly multiplying in the Tombigbee country, and he knew that the Americans had made acquisitions of new territory which would still further invite American emigration into the neighbourhood of the Creek Nation. All this he saw with alarm, because he was convinced that it boded ill to his people. With many others he feared that the race which held black men in a state of slavery would reduce red men to a similar condition as soon as their own numbers in the country should be great enough to render resistance useless. Convinced of this, Red Eagle believed that it was the part of wisdom to make a fight for freedom before it should be forever too late.

Tecumseh, finding in the young chief a man of the highest influence in the nation, whose prejudices, fears, and judgment combined to make him an advocate of war, took him at once into his councils, making him his confidant and principal fellow-worker. Red Eagle eagerly seconded Tecumseh's efforts, and his influence won many, especially of the young warriors, to the war party in the nation. His knowledge of the Creeks, too, enabled him to suggest methods of winning them which his visitor would not have thought of, probably. One of these was to work directly upon their imaginations, and to enlist their superstition on the side of war through prophets of their own, who, by continuous prophesyings, could do much to counteract the influence of the older Creek chiefs, most of whom were attached to the Americans, and being well-to-do were opposed to war, which might lose them their houses, lands, cattle, and negro slaves. The possession of property, even among partly savage men, is a strong conservative influence always.

Acting upon Red Eagle's hint, Tecumseh directed his prophet to "inspire" some Creeks with prophetic powers. The first man selected for this purpose was wisely chosen. He was a shrewd half-breed named Josiah Francis, a man whose great cunning and unscrupulousness fitted him admirably for the business of "prophet."

The prophet of the Shawnees took Francis to a cabin and shut him up alone for the space of ten days. During that time the inspiring was accomplished by the Shawnee, who danced and howled around the cabin, and performed all manner of rude gesticulations. At the end of the ten days he brought the new prophet forth, telling the people that he was now blind, but that very soon his sight—which may be said to have been taken away to be sharpened—would be restored to him, so improved that he could see all things that were to occur in the future.

Francis, of course, lent himself willingly to this imposture, and consented to be led about by the Shawnee prophet, stepping like a blind man who fears to stumble over obstacles. Suddenly he declared that he had received his vision, duly made over, with modern improvements and prophetic attachments.

Francis used his new powers both directly and by proxy in the interest of the war party, creating many other prophets to help him, among them Sinquista and High Head Jim; and the diligence with which all these workers for war carried on their prophesyings, pleadings, and speech-making increased the numbers of the war party, and added to the ill-feeling, which was already intense, between the Creeks who wished to make war and those who sought to keep the peace. The Creek nation was ripe for a civil war—a war of factions among themselves; it only needed a spark to create an explosion, and the spark was not long in coming, as we shall see.

Tecumseh, having secured so good a substitute for himself in Red Eagle, felt that his own presence was no longer needed in the Creek country. He accordingly took his departure for the north by a circuitous route, in order that he might visit the tribes on the Missouri River and in Illinois, and stir them up to hostility. He took with him the Creek chief Little Warrior, and thirty men of the nation. These Creeks accompanied him in all his wanderings until they reached Canada, where they remained a considerable time, receiving attentions of the most flattering kind from British officers and from the secret agents of the British. Upon their departure for the return journey, they were provided with letters which directed the British agents at Pensacola to provide the Creeks with arms and ammunition in abundance.

On their way back they committed an outrage which, although it had no direct bearing upon the quarrel among the Creeks at home, proved in the end to be the beginning of that civil war which grew into a war with the whites. In the Chickasaw country they murdered seven families, and making a prisoner of a Mrs. Crawley, carried her with them to their own country. This outrageous conduct was at once reported by the Chickasaw agent to Colonel Hawkins, the agent for the Creeks, and he immediately demanded the punishment of its perpetrators. Under the compact which existed between the Creeks and the government, the chiefs of the tribe were bound to comply with this demand, upon pain of bringing the responsibility for the misdeed upon the nation, and as we have said the majority of the chiefs were anxious to fulfil their duties and thus to preserve peace. Accordingly, a council of friendly chiefs determined to arrest Little Warrior's band and punish them. They sent two parties of warriors to do this, one under command of Chief McIntosh, and the other led by Captain Isaacs. These forest policemen speedily accomplished their mission, pursuing and fighting the offenders until all of them were put to death. This was in the spring of 1812.

Justice being satisfied, the Creeks might now have remained at peace with the whites if they had joined the older chiefs in wishing to do so; but unfortunately that which placated the whites only served to incense the war party among the Creeks against both the whites and the peaceful men of their own nation. Murders and other outrages occurred frequently. The men of the war party became truculent in their bearing, and matters were in a ferment throughout the nation. The prophets prophesied, and the orators made speeches denouncing the "peacefuls," as they called the Creeks who opposed war, as bitterly as they did the whites. The Alabamas were especially violent, probably in consequence of their close neighbourhood with Red Eagle, whose influence over them was almost without limit. They committed outrages especially designed to force the beginning of war, among other things killing a mail-carrier, seizing the United States mail and carrying it to Pensacola, where they robbed the bags of their contents.

Big Warrior, who had stood so firmly against Tecumseh's threats, still held out, but he was now thoroughly aroused. He invited the chiefs of the war party to a council, but they scorned to listen to his pleas for a hearing. Failing to bring them to him, he sent a messenger to them with his "talk," which was in these words:

> You are but a few Alabama people. You say that the Great Spirit visits you frequently; that he comes in the sun, and speaks to you; that the sun comes down just above your heads. Now we want to see and hear what you have seen and heard. Let us have the same proof, then we will believe. You have nothing to fear; the people who did the killing on the Ohio are put to death, and the law is satisfied.

This was a perfectly sensible, logical, reasonable talk, and for that reason it angered the men to whom it was sent. Men in a passion always resent reason when it condemns them or stands in the way of their purposes. The Alabamas answered Big Warrior's sensible proposition by putting his messenger to death. Thus the civil war among the Creeks, for it had become that now, went on. The peaceful Indians remained true to their allegiance, and fought their hostile brethren when occasion required, although they did what they could to avoid collisions with them.

In such a time as that even civilized men become disorderly, and the hostile Creeks grew daily more and more turbulent. They collected in parties and went upon marauding expeditions, sometimes sacking a plantation, sometimes murdering a party of emigrants, sometimes making a descent upon the dwellings of peaceful Creeks, and doing all manner of mischief.

The long-threatened war between the United States and Great Britain had been formally declared in the year 1812, and it was now the spring of 1813. The Americans at the beginning of the war had asserted their title to the town and harbour of Mobile, which, although a part of the territory ceded many years before to this country by the French, had until now been held by the Spanish. The affair was so well managed that the place was surrendered without bloodshed and occupied by the American forces; but its surrender served to increase the hostility of the Spanish in Florida, and although we were nominally at peace with Spain, the Spanish authorities at Pensacola, who had already done much to stir up Indian hostilities, lent themselves readily to the schemes of the British. During the latter part of August, 1812, they went so far as to permit a British force to land at Pensacola, take possession of the fort there, and make the place a base of military operations against us.

From the very beginning of the troubles the Indians had maintained communication with Pensacola, and parties of them went thither frequently to procure arms and ammunition, which were freely furnished. It was with one of these parties, on their return from Pensacola, that the first battle of the Creek war was fought. Of that we shall hear in another chapter. Meantime it is worth while to explain how the plans of the war party were discovered in time to save many lives.

A friendly half-breed, McNac by name, was driven from his home by one of the petty marauding parties spoken of a few pages back, and his cattle were carried to Pensacola by the marauders, and sold. After hiding in the swamps for some time, McNac at last ventured out at night to visit his home and see precisely what damage had been done. He was unlucky enough to meet High Head Jim at the head of a party of hostile Indians, and as there was no chance of safety either in flight or fight, McNac resorted to diplomacy, which in this case, as in many others, meant vigorous lying. He declared that he had abandoned his peaceful proclivities, and had made up his mind to join the war party. McNac appears to have had something like a genius for lying, as he succeeded in imposing his fabrications upon High Head Jim, who, suspicious and treacherous as he was, believed McNac implicitly, and confided to him the plan of the hostile Creeks. This plan was to kill Big Warrior, Captain Isaacs, McIntosh, Mad Dragon's Son, and the other friendly chiefs, before going finally upon the war-path, and, having thus deprived the friendly Creeks of their leaders, to compel them to join in the war upon the Americans. Then, High Head Jim said, the war would begin by simultaneous attacks upon the various settlements. Having exterminated the whites upon their borders, they were to march in three columns against the people of Tennessee, Georgia, and Mississippi, receiving assistance from the Choctaws and the Cherokees.

McNac bore this information at once to the intended victims, and thus enabled them to secure their safety in various ways; but the civil war increased in its fury. The hostile bands still confined themselves as yet chiefly to attacks upon the peaceful members of their own nation, destroying their houses, killing or driving off their cattle, and stealing whatever portable property they possessed.

Colonel Hawkins still hoped for peace, rather unreasonably, it must be confessed, and avoided interference as far as possible; but he extended protection to Big Warrior, and with the assistance of a force of friendly Creeks rescued that chieftain and escorted him to a place of safety.

In such a state of affairs, of course, a collision between the whites and the Indians was inevitable, and when it came, as will be related in the next chapter, the Creek war of 1813 was begun.

CHAPTER 6

The Battle of Burnt Corn

In the month of July, 1813, Peter McQueen, High Head Jim, and the Prophet Francis, having collected a large amount of plunder in their descents upon the homes of peaceful Indians and the plantations of half-breeds, sought a market for their booty. Collecting their followers to the number of about three hundred men, they loaded a number of pack-horses, and set out for Pensacola, driving a herd of stolen cattle before them. It was their purpose to exchange these things at Pensacola for arms, ammunition, whiskey, and whatever else they wanted; and combining pleasure with business, they amused themselves on the route by burning villages and committing murders upon Indians who persisted in their friendship for the whites.

Meantime the white people had at last become thoroughly alarmed. The news which McNac brought of his conversation with High Head Jim convinced even the most sceptical that a war of greater or smaller proportions was at hand, and it was the conviction of the wisest men among them that the best way to save themselves from impending destruction was to strike in time. The British had now begun seriously to threaten a descent upon the south-west, and it seemed to be more than probable that the savages were only delaying their general outbreak until their allies the British should appear somewhere upon the coast, and force the militia of the Tensaw and Tombigbee settlements to march away to meet them. Then the country would be defenceless, and the Indians could easily exterminate all that remained of the white population.

The pioneers who lived in that part of the country were brave, hardy, and resolute men, and they no sooner saw their danger distinctly than they took up arms with which to defend themselves. They resolved to assert their resolution by attacking not the Indian towns, but the roving parties of Indian outlaws who were bringing the war about. If they could crush these, punishing them effectually, they thought, the great body of the Creeks would think twice before deciding to make the contemplated war.

Accordingly a summons was sent out for volunteers. About two hundred men, or nearly that number, some of them white men, some half-breeds, and some friendly Indians, promptly answered the call. Among them was Captain Samuel Dale, better known in history as Sam Dale, the hero of the canoe fight, one of the strangest and most desperate affairs of the war, some account of which will be given in its proper place.

This little army was commanded by Colonel Caller, assisted by one lieutenant-colonel, four majors, and more captains and lieutenants than have been counted. Deducting these from the total force, we are led to the conviction that there must have been an average of about one officer to every two men; but even this enormous proportion of officers did not prevent the men from behaving badly in the presence of the enemy and getting sharply beaten, as will be related presently.

When the several companies composing this expedition were brought together, the line of march was taken toward Pensacola, with the purpose of encountering Peter McQueen and his force on their return. On the morning of July 27th, 1813, the advance scouts came in and reported that McQueen's force was encamped upon Burnt Corn Creek, just in advance of Caller's column, and that officer promptly determined to attack them.

Forming his men in line he advanced cautiously through the reeds until the Indian camp lay just below. Then, with a yell, the men dashed forward to the charge, and after a few moments' resistance the surprised and beaten Indians abandoned their camp with its horses and its rich stores of ammunition and food, and fled precipitately to the creek, by which the camp was encircled except upon the side from which the white men came. Dale, who was a born Indian fighter, Captain Dixon Bailey, and Captain Smoot—who were also resolute men and good officers, Bailey being an educated half-breed—saw at a glance that to pursue the flying savages was to crush them utterly; and they therefore led their men, some seventy-five or eighty in number, forward, and crowded the Indians as closely as possible. Had they been promptly supported, McQueen's force would have been utterly destroyed, and there might have been no Creek war for us to write and read about. Unluckily the other officers were less wise than Dale and Bailey and Smoot. When the Indians gave way and ran, leaving their camp with its pack-horses loaded with goods, the officers and men of the main body supposed that their work was done. Instead of joining in the pursuit, they broke their ranks, threw down their arms, and busied themselves securing the plunder.

Peter McQueen was a shrewd fellow in his way, and he was not long in discovering the weakness of the force which had followed him to the creek. Rallying his men he gave them battle, and began pressing them back. Colonel Caller, who was leading the advance, instead of ordering his main body to the front, as a more experienced officer would have done, determined to fall back upon them as a reserve. Dale, Smoot, and Bailey could have maintained their position while waiting for the reinforcements to come up, but when ordered to fall back upon the main body, their brave but untrained and inexperienced men retreated rather hastily. The men of the main body, having broken ranks to plunder, were in no condition to resist panic, and seeing the advance companies retreating, with the yelling Indians at their heels, they fled precipitately. Caller, Dale, Bailey, and Smoot tried to rally them, but succeeded only in getting eighty men into line. This small force, commanded by their brave officers, made a desperate stand, and brought the advancing savages to a halt. Dale was severely wounded, but he fought on in spite of his suffering and his weakness. Finally, seeing that they were overmatched and that their comrades had abandoned them to their fate, the little band retreated, fighting as they went, until at last the Indians abandoned the pursuit. Some of the Americans went home, others became lost and were found, nearly dead with fatigue and starvation, about a fortnight later.

Thus ended the battle of Burnt Corn. It was lost to the white men solely by the misconduct of officers and men, but that misconduct was the result of inexperience and a want of discipline, not of cowardice or any lack of manhood.

The Indians were badly hurt. Their losses, though not known definitely, are known to have been greater than those of the whites, of whom only two were killed and fifteen wounded. They had lost their pack-horses, and nearly all the fruits of their journey to Pensacola, so that they were forced to return to that post to procure fresh supplies.

The affair was a much more serious disaster to the whites, however, than at first appeared. The expedition had been undertaken for the purpose of destroying McQueen's party, and thereby intimidating the war-inclined Creeks. In that it had utterly failed. The Creeks were victors, though they had suffered loss. Their victory encouraged them, and their losses still further incensed them. The war which before was threatened was now actually begun. The first battle had been fought, and others must follow of necessity. The Creeks believed themselves to be able to exterminate the whites, and they were now determined to do so.

In this determination they were strengthened not merely by the general countenance given to them at Pensacola, but by very specific and urgent advice from the British and Spanish officers there, who, as we learn from official documents, urged the Creeks to make the war at once, saying:

> If they (the Americans) prove too hard for you, send your women and children to Pensacola and we will send them to Havana; and if you should be compelled to fly yourselves, and the Americans should prove too hard for both of us, there are vessels enough to take us all off together.

CHAPTER 7

Red Eagle's Attempt to Abandon His Party

Red Eagle, as we have already related, was the most active and efficient leader of the war party during all the time of preparation. At last the war which he had so earnestly sought to bring about had come, but it had not come in the way in which he had hoped, and Red Eagle hesitated.

In the first place the war had come too soon. Red Eagle was too shrewd and too well informed to believe the predictions of his prophets Sinquista and Francis, who told the Creeks that if they would completely abandon those things which they had learned of the whites and become utter savages, not one of them should be killed in the war; that the Great Spirit would rain down fire upon the whites, create quagmires in their path, cause the earth to open and swallow them, and draw charmed circles around the camps of the Creeks, into which no white man could come without immediately falling down dead. Like many another shrewd leader, Red Eagle was willing to make use of this sort of appeals to superstition, while he was himself unaffected by them. He saw clearly enough that the white men were strong, because he knew that their numbers and resources were not limited by what he could see. He knew that armies would come from other quarters of the country to aid the settlers on the Tombigbee River and in the Tensaw settlement. Therefore he did not wish to undertake what he knew would be a severe contest, single-handed. He wanted to wait until Tecumseh, who had promised to return, should come; he was disposed to wait also for the British to land a force somewhere on the coast before beginning the war.

Moreover, his schemes and his advocacy of war had been from the first founded upon his conviction that the friendship of the Creeks and half-breeds in the lower towns for the whites would give way when they should see that the war was inevitable. He had sought to bring about a war in which the whole Creek nation should be united against the whites; what he had brought about was a very different affair. He now saw that the friendliness of the people of the lower towns, who were his nearest friends and kinsmen, including his brother, Jack Weatherford, and his half-brother, David Tait, was much more firmly fixed than he had imagined. He had supposed that it was merely the indisposition of rich men to imperil their property by bringing on a state of war; he now knew that it was a fixed purpose to remain at peace with the white men, and even to join them in fighting the Creeks whenever the war should come. If he had cherished a doubt of this so long, he had proof of it in the presence of some of these friends of his in the American force at the battle of Burnt Corn, whither they had gone as volunteers.

All this put a totally different face upon matters. Red Eagle was eager for a war between the Creeks and whites, but a war between a part of the Creeks on the one hand, and the rest of the Creeks with the whites on the other, a war in which he must fight his own brothers and his nearest friends, was a very different and much less attractive affair.

There was still another cause of Red Eagle's hesitation at this time—perhaps a stronger cause than either of the others. He was in love, and his sweetheart was among the people whom he must fight if he fought at all. He was a rich planter, and lived at this time on a fine place near the Holy Ground, and being a young widower he had conceived a passionate fancy for one Lucy Cornells, a young girl of mixed Indian and white blood, who has been described by persons who knew her as very attractive and beautiful. However that may be, it is certain that Red Eagle's devotion to her was profound.

This girl's father, when McNac's discovery of the Indian plans spread consternation through the settlements, fled with his daughter to the Tensaw country and took refuge in Fort Mims; and Red Eagle had thus a sweetheart added to the list of persons near and dear to him, whose lives he must put in danger if he went to war. Anticipating the events of this history somewhat, it may as well be added here that Red Eagle's love for this maiden prompted him, when he was about to attack Fort Mims, to give secret warning to her father, as is believed upon evidence accepted at the time as satisfactory. Cornells left the fort before the attack, and although he remained with the whites and fought with them in the war, Red Eagle was permitted to carry off his daughter to the nation.

Let us return to the time of which we write in this chapter. All these things were strong inducements to Red Eagle to abandon his warlike purposes, but it was now too late for him to still the storm he had raised. Had he now preached peace among his warlike followers, his life would not have been worth a day's purchase.

He kept his own counsel, and in his perplexity determined, about the time of the battle of Burnt Corn, to seek the advice of his brother, Jack Weatherford, and his half-brother, David Tait. Making his way to their places on Little River, he laid the whole case before his relatives. They advised him secretly to remove his family, his negroes, and so much of his live-stock as might be, to their plantations, which lay within the friendly district, and, quitting the nation, to remain quietly with them until the troubles should come to an end, taking no part in the war on either side.

After reflecting upon the matter, Red Eagle determined to act upon this advice; and thus the Creeks were very near losing the services of that chieftain whose genius alone enabled them to maintain their war with any hope of success. When Red Eagle returned to his plantation to put this plan into operation, however, he found that it was now too late. Knowing at least some of the reasons their chief had for abandoning his support of their cause, some of the hostile Creeks had visited his house in his absence, and had seized upon his children and his negroes, holding them as hostages for his fidelity. They plainly told him of their doubts of him, and threatened to kill his children if he should falter for a moment.

There was nothing left for him to do but yield to his fate, and boldly lead his men to battle against the foes whom he cordially hated. His Rubicon was crossed, his die was cast, and there was no possibility of retreat.

CHAPTER 8

Claiborne and Red Eagle

If Weatherford was at last ready to enter upon the long-contemplated war, so too the white people at last began to understand that their hopes of a reconciliation of some kind with the Creeks were delusive, and they began to take measures for their defence. Even yet, however, they seem to have had no adequate conception of the real nature and extent of the storm that was brewing. Their measures of defence were not proportioned to the need, were not of the right kind, except in part, and were carried forward lazily, listlessly, and apparently with a deep-seated conviction that, after all, the making of preparation might be a useless waste of labour in anticipation of a danger which might never come.

There can be little doubt that if these people had fully understood their own situation they could and would have saved themselves by adopting a vigorous offensive policy from the outset. Colonel Caller's expedition to Burnt Corn was a type and example of what they ought to have attempted. They should have struck the first blows, and should have followed them up as rapidly as possible. If they had understood their own situation they would probably have done this. They would have organized the whole population into an army, and if they had done this they might almost certainly have conquered a peace with comparatively small loss to themselves before Weatherford had time to bring his roving parties together for the contest.

Instead of this, however, the only attempt that was made to meet hostility half-way—the Burnt Corn expedition—ended in failure, and the men who had undertaken it dispersed to their homes. It was now too late for a policy of offensive defence. The battle of

Burnt Corn was followed by an immediate concentration of the hostile Creeks, and the most that could be done by the whites to avert the threatened destruction was to fortify certain central posts and send messengers for assistance.

The method of fortifying was the same in all cases, with such variations of detail as the nature of the ground, the number of men engaged in the construction of the works, and the other circumstances of each case rendered necessary. In general plan the so-called forts were nearly square, the most elaborate of them being constructed upon the plan of Fort Mims, which is represented on another page. Whatever their form was, they were made of timbers set on end in the ground, as close together as possible, forming a close and high wall, pierced with port-holes for the use of riflemen. Heavy gates were provided, and within the enclosure strong block-houses were built, in which a stout resistance could be made even after the outer works should be carried.

There were more than a score of these forts in different parts of the settlements. In that part of the peninsula formed by the Alabama and Tombigbee rivers which now constitutes Clarke County, Alabama, there were stockades built, which were known as Fort Glass, Fort Sinquefield, etc., each taking its name from the owner of the place fortified.

Into these forts the people now began to flock in anticipation of a general outbreak; and they were none too soon, as Weatherford had already collected his men in considerable numbers. The principal fort was on the plantation of one Samuel Mims, a rich Indian or man of mixed blood, who lived on the little lake called Tensaw, or Tensas, as it is now sometimes spelled on the maps, which lies within about a mile of the Alabama River, a few miles above the confluence of that river with the Tombigbee. Mims's place was near the high-road which led to Mims's ferry, and hence was a natural centre of the neighbourhood.

Mims and his neighbours, with the help of a number of half-breed refugees from the Creek nation, constructed there a large stockade fortress, and the people of the surrounding country, white, black, red, and mixed, congregated there for safety.

Meantime the appearance of a British fleet off the coast had awakened the government to the danger in which Mobile lay, and on the 28th of June, 1813, Brigadier-General Ferdinand L. Claiborne, a distinguished soldier who had won a fine reputation in the Indian wars of the North-west, was ordered, with what force he had, to march from the post of Baton Rouge to Fort Stoddard, a military station on the Mobile River, not far below the confluence of the Alabama and Tombigbee rivers.

Upon receiving this order General Claiborne made application for the necessary funds and supplies, but the quartermaster could put no more than two hundred dollars into his army chest—a sum wholly inadequate to the purpose. But Claiborne was not a man to permit small obstacles to interfere with affairs of importance. He borrowed the necessary funds upon his personal credit, giving a mortgage upon his property as security, and boldly set out with his little army. It is worth while to note in passing that, in consequence of the loss of vouchers for his expenditures upon the expedition, General Claiborne's patriotic act cost him the whole amount borrowed, his property being sold after his death, as we learn from a note in Pickett's History of Alabama, to satisfy the mortgage.

Arriving at Fort Stoddard with his army of seven hundred men on the thirtieth day of July, General Claiborne at once sought the fullest and most trustworthy information to be had with respect to the condition of the country, the forces and designs of the Indians, and the strength and situation of the various forts.

Having thus made himself master of the conditions of the problem which he was set to solve, he distributed his forces and the volunteers who were at command, among the various stockade posts in such a way as to give the best protection he could to every part of the country.

To Fort Mims he sent Major Beasley, with one hundred and seventy-five men, who, with seventy militiamen already there, swelled the force at that post to two hundred and forty-five fighting men. Major Beasley, upon taking command, organized his raw troops into something resembling a battalion, and strengthened the fort by erecting a second line of picketing outside the original gates.

Believing the post to be strong enough to spare a part of the force under his command, Major Beasley sent detachments to various other and weaker posts, acting upon the principle of protecting all points, which had governed General Claiborne.

Besides the troops, who were simply all the men in the fort, every man capable of shooting a gun being enrolled as a soldier, there were women and children at Fort Mims, who had fled thither from the country for protection, so that the total number of persons there exceeded five hundred; the exact number is differently stated by different writers, but the most trustworthy account, drawn from several original sources, places the population of the place at five hundred and fifty-three souls. The lives of all these people were committed to the keeping of Major Beasley, who was clothed with ample authority, and free from embarrassing dictation or interference of any kind. His fort was a strong one, and in sending away some of his men to assist the garrisons of other posts he himself testified that the force which remained was sufficient for the need. His failure to use these means effectually for the protection of the lives over which he was set as guardian was clearly inexcusable, and although he bravely sacrificed his own life in an attempt to retrieve his fault, he could do nothing to undo its terrible consequences. His fault was not cowardice, but a lack of caution, an utter and inexcusable lack of that prudence and foresight which are as indispensable in a commander as personal courage itself.

It appears that alarms were frequent in the fort, as was to be expected in a place full of women and children, credulous negroes, and excited militiamen. These alarms Beasley reported to General Claiborne, and in doing so he probably gave that capable and experienced officer some hint of his own lack of prudence. At any rate, General Claiborne thought it necessary to issue a general order to Major Beasley, directing him to strengthen his works, use caution in the conduct of affairs, and neglect no means of making the safety of the fort certain. The order ended with this significant sentence:

To respect an enemy and prepare in the best possible way to meet him, is the certain means to insure success.

All the work done by Major Beasley to strengthen the works was done in obedience to special orders from Claiborne, and even what he specifically ordered done appears to have been done only in part. He directed Major Beasley, for one thing, to build two additional block-houses, but that officer contented himself with beginning to build one, which was never finished.

With matters in Fort Mims, and the results of Major Beasley's

Fort Mims

management there, we shall have to do in another chapter. We have first to look at the general situation of affairs as they stood during August, 1813, before Weatherford—for by that name, rather than Red Eagle, he is known to the history of what followed—struck his first tremendous blow.

Weatherford had collected his men in the upper towns, and was now moving down the river, managing his advance very skilfully, after the manner of regularly educated military men. In small affairs the Indian general followed the tactics of his race, depending upon cunning and silent creeping for the concealment of his movements, but he was too able an officer to fall into the mistake of supposing that an army could be advanced in this way for a long distance in secret. He knew that his movements would be watched very closely and promptly reported. He therefore resorted to strategy— or rather to sound methods of grand tactics—as a means of concealing, not the fact that he was advancing, but the real direction and objective point of his advance. He moved southward, taking care to make demonstrations upon his flank which were calculated to deceive his enemy. He threatened the settlements in the peninsula, and constantly kept up a front of observation in a direction different from that in which his main body was actually moving. In this way he managed to advance to McGirth's plantation, on the Alabama River, in the neighbourhood of the place where the town of Claiborne now stands, without revealing the purpose of his advance, and as this halting point was one at which his presence seemed to threaten an attack upon Fort Glass, Fort Sinquefield, and the other posts in what is now Clarke County, his real purpose was still effectually concealed.

Meantime General Claiborne was not disposed to lie still and permit his wily adversary to determine the course of the campaign. We said in the beginning of this chapter that by a timely resort to offensive measures the settlers might have averted a general war. It was now General Claiborne's opinion that with the troops at command a policy of this kind offered even yet the best prospect of success. Even before he had finished his defensive preparations he planned an offensive campaign, which he was confident of his ability to execute, while he was equally confident that its execution would save a very much severer effort in future.

On the 2nd of August, 1813, he wrote to his commanding general, explaining the situation, and adding these words:

> If you will authorize my entering the Creek nation, I will do so in ten days after the junction of the Seventh Regiment, and if I am not disappointed, will give to our frontiers peace, and to the government any portion of the Creek country they please. Some force ought to enter the nation before they systematize and are fully prepared for war. With one thousand men and your authority to march immediately, I pledge myself to burn any town in the Creek nation. Three months hence it might be difficult for three thousand to effect what can be done with a third of the number at present. They gain strength, and their munitions of war enlarge every day.

How accurately General Claiborne estimated the difficulties which delay would produce will be abundantly seen as we follow the course of the campaign. There can be little reasonable doubt that the blow which this gallant and enterprising officer wished to strike then would have saved many hundreds of lives on both sides, if he had been permitted to carry his plan into effect; but there was a difficulty in the way—the Creeks had not yet openly attacked the white settlements beyond their border, and until they did so the commanding general had no authority to permit his troops to invade the nation.

CHAPTER 9

Red Eagle Before Fort Mims

Now that it was determined that General Claiborne should not invade the Creek country and crush Weatherford before that chieftain's forces should be fully gathered and fully armed, there was nothing for General Claiborne to do but wait the attack of his Indian adversary with what patience he could, taking care to neglect no precaution which might help to secure safety. He visited all the forts one after another, inspected them, and gave minute and careful instructions for their strengthening, everywhere cautioning their commanders to beware of surprise, and to avoid the danger of falling into careless habits. He knew the Indians well, and knew that they would seek with great care to make their first attack unexpectedly, and also that they would bring as heavy a force as possible to bear upon the point of attack. He knew the temper of the militiamen too, and seems to have specially feared that they would be lulled into a dangerous feeling of security by delay and by repeated false alarms.

Against all of these dangers this thoroughly capable commander continually cautioned his subordinate officers to whom he committed the command of the several forts. Had his warnings been duly heeded, a result far different from that which we shall have to record would have followed.

Having delivered his orders, General Claiborne went to the most exposed point, a small fort about sixty miles further into the Indian country, confidently believing that Red Eagle would make his first attack there, with a view of freeing the country of white men before making a decided advance against any of the forts near the confluence of the two rivers. In this he erred, as the event

56

showed, but the error was one which no foresight or judgment could have avoided. Red Eagle was a bold and a shrewd warrior, and when he was free to choose his time and place of attack, as he was at this time, it was simply impossible to conjecture with accuracy where or when he would strike. He was like the lightning, dealing his blows without a hint, in advance, of their object. General Claiborne having no means of ascertaining what his adversary would do, and no chance to guess, simply went to the front as a brave commander should.

Meantime Major Beasley soon began to neglect proper precautions. He left the new blockhouse and the new line of picketing unfinished, although he had idle men in plenty who could have completed them with very little effort. The accounts which have been given of the life in the fort indicate that the commander was utterly wanting in the first qualification of an officer for command—namely, a due regard for discipline. He had raw troops under his command—troops whose efficiency as soldiers would have been more than doubled during those days of inaction and waiting if daily or twice daily drills had been ordered and anything like discipline or military order maintained. That a commander entrusted with the charge of so important a fort, especially with the lives of so many helpless women and children committed to his care, should have neglected so good an opportunity to convert his raw recruits into drilled and disciplined soldiers, would scarcely be credible if the fact were not fully attested.

Instead of improving the precious days of waiting in this way, Major Beasley wholly relaxed the reins of discipline. The men gave themselves up to roistering, card-playing, and uproarious fun-making.

About this time a negro, whom Weatherford had captured near McGirth's plantation, escaped, and, making his way to Fort Mims, informed Major Beasley of the whereabouts of the Indian force, telling him also that the Indian chieftain had made careful inquiries about this particular fort, its strength, the number of persons in it, and other details, his anxiety about which indicated his purpose to attack the post. Major Beasley sent out scouting parties; but as they discovered no Indians in the neighbourhood he appears immediately to have relapsed into his former state of listlessness. He did not respect his enemy, as Claiborne had so earnestly warned him to do. The men, calling the negro from McGirth's plantation a liar, returned to their frolics and their idleness.

Red Eagle, wiser than his enemy, respected him, and advanced so cautiously that he actually placed his army within striking distance of the fort without Beasley's knowledge, and concealed his men so adroitly that Beasley's scouting parties failed to discover them. Beasley was as brave a man as Red Eagle, but Red Eagle had the other qualities of a soldier—sagacity, caution, tireless watchfulness—which Beasley lacked; in a contest between the two as commanders, Red Eagle was Beasley's master. One day, while Red Eagle was thus hovering about the fort, watching it as a cat watches its prey, two negroes, who had been guarding some cattle, ran in great terror to the fort, and reported that they had seen Indians in the immediate neighbourhood. Major Beasley at once sent a body of horsemen under command of Captain Middleton to ascertain the facts of the case. Captain Middleton, accompanied by the negroes, went to the spot where they said they had seen the savages; finding no Indians there, Captain Middleton, who appears to have thought that Indians are like trees, staying in one place, returned to the fort and reported that a false alarm had been given. The poor negroes were denounced as liars, and one of them was flogged for having given a false alarm. The other was saved for a while by the intercession of his master, but he was afterward arraigned again, his master's consent having been gained by Major Beasley's threat to expel him and his family from the fort if he persisted in his refusal; and it is upon record that when the fort was attacked the negro was standing tied, and awaiting his flogging.

This incident is mentioned here in illustration of the unaccountable folly of Major Beasley. The writers who have recorded the facts of this officer's behaviour have touched them as lightly as possible, sparing him probably because he fought manfully and fell at his post at last; but it is impossible to regard his conduct with any thing like respect or even patience. His carelessness was a crime, and history must condemn it as such. Charged with the duty of defending an important post, he neglected the most essential measures of defence; entrusted with the lives of more than five hundred persons, he carelessly, criminally, permitted them to

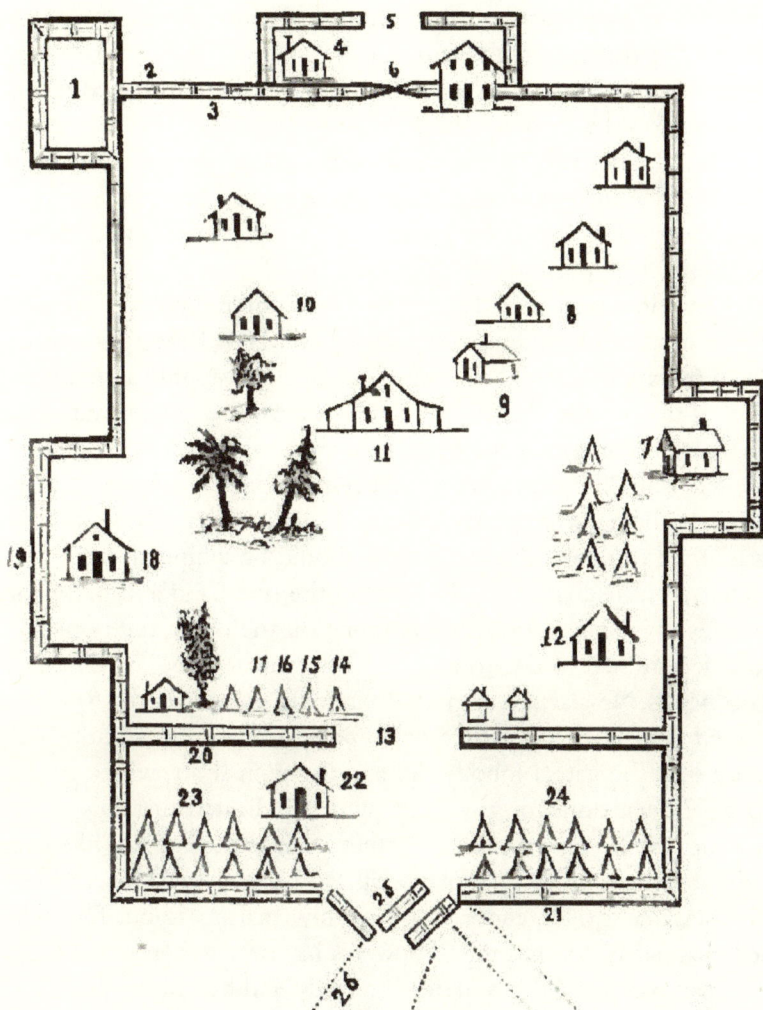

Fort Mims (interior)

be butchered. We have already seen that he neglected discipline in the fort; he neglected also to surround the fort, as he should have done, with a cordon of picket-guards, who might have been so placed that ample warning would have been given of the approach of the enemy. Instead of that, he actually subjected the negroes who gave warning to ignominious punishment, and, most incredible thing of all, permitted the gates of the fort to stand open until the accumulation of sand at their base rendered it impossible to shut them promptly!

The alarm given by the negroes was given on the 29th day of August. The next morning the negro who had been flogged was again sent out to guard the cattle, and his companion was detained to receive his punishment.

Meantime Red Eagle lay within a few hundred yards of the fort, at the head of a thousand warriors. While Major Beasley was using his authority to compel the negro's master to consent to the infliction of the penalty, Red Eagle and his men were quietly watching the fort, looking in at the open gate and making ready to destroy the garrison. The negro who had been whipped again saw the Indians, he being where a picket-guard ought to have been; but he was afraid to report the fact lest he should be whipped again, and so between his fear of the Indians on the one hand and of Major Beasley's peculiar notions of discipline on the other, the poor fellow determined to flee to another fort, two or three miles east of Fort Mims. No alarm was given, therefore. Nobody in the fort suspected Red Eagle's presence or prepared to meet his assault. Nobody shut the gate. Nobody did any thing, in short, which ought to have been done, or any thing which indicated that this was a fort, or that its commander knew that a war existed or was likely to exist anywhere on earth. Worst of all, Red Eagle lay there watching his prey like a tiger, and seeing just how matters stood. The able commander of the red men knew his business and attended to it. His plan was formed, his men were ready, and he only awaited the coming of the right moment to spring upon his unsuspecting prey. It was nearly noon, and it was the most critical hour of the war.

CHAPTER 10

The Massacre at Fort Mims

The accounts of what followed, which are given in the various books that treat the subject, are for the most part very meagre, and upon one or two points of minor importance they conflict with each other. Luckily, we have one account which is much more minute than any other, and at the same time is entirely trustworthy. This account is found in Mr. A. J. Pickett's History of Alabama, a work remarkable for the diligence of research upon which it is founded, the author having been at great pains to gather details from the survivors of the various historical events of which he writes. Mr. Pickett had access to the private papers of General Claiborne, and to several survivors of the Fort Mims affair, and from these sources he gathered a mass of particulars which no other writer upon the subject had within reach. In writing here of the affair, we must depend mainly upon Mr. Pickett's pages for all matters of detail.

We left Red Eagle at the head of his men, within a short distance of the fort, quietly contemplating it. His prey was apparently within his grasp and his men were ready, but still Red Eagle waited, repressing the eagerness of his followers sternly. The people in the fort were singing, playing games, and occupying themselves in every way but the soldierly one. They were not on the alert—they were completely off their guard. Apparently the time had come to strike, but Red Eagle knew his business, and waited. He knew that to take a stockade fortress without the aid of artillery he must surprise the garrison completely, and this was what he sought to do by delay.

Noon came, and with it came the drum for dinner. That was

61

the signal Red Eagle had been waiting for. It was not enough that the garrison should be listlessly off guard. Red Eagle wished them to be occupied with something else, and now they were going to dinner. Giving them time enough collect for that purpose, the Indian commander advanced his line, doing so quietly, contrary to the Indian habit. He was determined to make the surprise as complete as possible. In this way the Indian line, running rapidly forward, reached a point within thirty yards of the open gates before their approach was discovered by anybody within. Then the few men who happened to be near enough made an attempt to close the gate; but it was too late, even if the accumulated sand at its foot had not prevented. The Indians rushed in pell-mell, and almost in the instant of discovering their presence Major Beasley learned that they were already within the outer lines of his defensive works.

Luckily there was a second line of picketing at this point, partly completed, which prevented the immediate passage of the Indians to all parts of the fort, and gave the whites a defensive work from which to fight their foes. Major Beasley was at last awake to the reality of the danger of which Claiborne had warned him repeatedly, his last warning having come in a letter which Beasley had received only the day before, and to which he had replied that he was prepared to repel the attack of any force which might come against his fortress. If he had scorned this danger culpably, and had neglected to provide against it as he should have done, he at least did what a brave man could to repel it, now that it had come. He was among the first to confront the enemy, and among the first to fall, mortally wounded. He rejected all offers of assistance and refused to be carried into the interior of the fort, preferring to remain where he was to animate the troops by his presence and to direct their operations. He continued thus to command them until the breath left his body.

The fighting was terrible. It was not two bodies of troops struggling for possession of some strategic point, but a horde of savages battling with a devoted band of white men in a struggle the only issue of which was death. The savages fought not to conquer but to kill the whites, every one, women and children as well as men; and the whites fought with the desperation of doomed men whose only chance of life was in victory. It was hand-to-hand fighting, too. It was fighting with knives and tomahawks and clubbed guns. Men grappled with each other, to relinquish their hold only in death.

Several Indian prophets were among the first of the savages to fall, and for a time their death spread consternation among their followers. These prophets had confidently told the Indians that their sacred bodies were invulnerable; that the bullets of white men would split upon them, doing no harm. When they went down before the first volley, therefore, the utter failure of their prophecy caused the Indians to lose faith in the cause, and they were ready like children to abandon it in their fright. Red Eagle was a man of different mettle. He had used these wretched false prophets to aid him in stirring the enthusiasm of the Creeks, but he had never believed their silly pretences. With such a commander the Creeks soon recovered their courage, and the fight went on.

Although Weatherford had gained a great advantage by his tactics of surprise and sudden onset, his task was still a very arduous one. He had possession of the outer gates, but the whites were still entrenched, and he must dislodge them—an undertaking which subjected him to heavy loss of men. Everybody within the fort who could shoot a gun or strike a blow with axe or club was engaged in the fight. Weatherford, like the general of real genius that he was, sent some of his men to threaten the other sides of the fort, thereby compelling the whites to distribute their force all around the enclosure, and thus to weaken the defence at the main point of attack. Captain Middleton had charge of the eastern side, and fell at his post. Captain Jack fought desperately on the southern face, and Lieutenant Randon on the west. Fortunately—if we may call any thing fortunate about an affair which ended in utter misfortune— the northern face of the fort, against which Weatherford hurled his men in greatest numbers and with greatest desperation, was defended by Captain Dixon Bailey, a man of mixed blood, who, it will be remembered, distinguished himself in the battle of Burnt Corn, and who seems to have had some of the qualities of an able commander. He saw and tried to make use of one chance of success. He knew and told his men that the force of an Indian attack was greatest in its beginning; that unless success crowned their efforts Indians were apt to weary of their work after a little while. He urged his followers, therefore, to fight with determination and with hope. He urged every non-combatant who could do so to join in the defence, and even some of the women did so. His judgment of the Indian character was right, and it was presently vindicated by the conduct of the savages, who relaxed their efforts to take the fort, and began making off with what plunder they could secure. But Red Eagle was there; and his presence was a factor for which Captain Bailey had not made due allowance. Riding after the retreating bands he quickly drove them back, and stimulated his forces to renewed exertions of the most desperate character.

Then Captain Bailey saw that his hope had been made vain by the resolution of this commander and by his genius for controlling men. It was now three o'clock, and the battle had lasted three hours. Captain Bailey seeing no chance for its cessation by the failure of savage determination, resolved to abandon the defences, and marching boldly out, attempt to cut a way through Red Eagle's hosts to Fort Pierce, a few miles distant. From this attempt he was restrained only by force.

The savages were now steadily gaining ground. One point after another was abandoned by the whites, whose numbers were rapidly diminishing. The savages fell as fast as the whites did, or even faster, but as they greatly outnumbered their entrenched foes they could afford this. Deducting the women and children from the whole number of people in the fort, it will be seen that the savages—whose force was estimated variously at from one thousand to fifteen hundred fighting men—outnumbered the fighting men of the fort at least three to one, and perhaps even as greatly as six or seven to one. With the fall of each white man, therefore, the relative superiority of the Indians was increased, even though two or three of the assailants should fall at the same time.

Little by little the fort yielded. From one defensive point to another the various bands of white men were driven, fighting as they went, and contesting every inch of the assailants' advance. Two brothers of Captain Dixon Bailey, James and Daniel Bailey, went with some other men into Mims's house, and piercing the roof with port-holes did excellent work upon bodies of savages who were protected by barriers of various kinds against the fire of men on the ground. To silence their fire some of the Indians shot burning arrows into the shingles of the house and succeeded in setting it on fire. They also fired several other buildings, and the poor people who still remained alive were now driven to their last place of refuge, a small enclosure around the loom house, called in the fort the bastion. From every quarter the warning cry "To the bastion!" went up, and very soon the small enclosure was so full of people that there was scarcely room for any one to move. Meantime the fire was gaining on every hand. Around the burning houses demoniac savages danced and shrieked and howled, while the women and children within the burning buildings could do nothing but wring their hands and commit themselves to heaven while awaiting certain and horrible destruction.

Red Eagle was a soldier, not a butcher; and now that his victory was secure he sought to stop the bloodshed and spare the lives of the helpless people who remained; he called upon his warriors to desist and to receive the survivors as prisoners, but the yelling savages would not listen to him. He attempted to assert his authority and compel them to stop the carnage, but the authority which he was able to wield in setting these savages on, failed utterly when he tried to call them off. When he thus sought to save the lives of white men and women and children, his followers remembered that he had not long before tried to withdraw altogether from the war, and with loud shrieks of anger they now turned upon him, threatening to put him to death if he should further plead for mercy. He could do nothing but submit, and turn away in horror from the sight of the brutal slaughter which he had made possible. Mounting his superb black horse he rode away, resolved to have at least no personal share in the horrible butchery.

The few remaining people in the fort were now shut up in a slaughter-pen. A few of them cut a hole through the outer picketing and made a dash for life. Of these about twenty escaped in different directions, and in one way or another managed after many hardships to reach other forts. All the rest of the people in the fort were butchered, except a few negroes kept by the savages as slaves, and one half-breed family, of whom we shall hear more presently.

The persons who escaped by flight were Dr. Thomas G. Holmes, a negro woman named Hester, a friendly Indian named

65

Socca, Lieutenant Peter Randon, Josiah Fletcher, Sergeant Matthews, Martin Rigdon, Samuel Smith, a half-breed, Joseph Perry, Jesse Steadham, Edward Steadham, John Horen, Lieutenant W. R. Chambers, two men named Mourrice and Jones, and some others whose names have not come down to us.

Thus ended the battle of Fort Mims, in some respects the most remarkable battle between Indians and white men of which history anywhere tells us. It had lasted for five hours without cessation, a most unusual thing in Indian warfare, which consists chiefly of sudden onsets that are not long persisted in if stoutly resisted. At Fort Mims the assault was kept up, in the face of desperate resistance, from noon until nearly sunset—a persistence due solely to the fact that the savages were for once commanded by a real soldier, who possessed the qualities of an able and determined general. The Indians here, as everywhere else, were disposed after a while, as has been said, to relinquish their purpose and content themselves with what they had accomplished in the way of destruction, but, as we have seen, Red Eagle sternly drove them back into battle, and succeeded in carrying the fort. If there were nothing else in his career to prove his title to respect as a really able military man, his management of this Fort Mims affair would sufficiently establish his claim.

CHAPTER 11

Incidents of the Fort Mims Affair

It was Dr. Thomas G. Holmes who planned the sortie by which
the persons named in the last chapter made their escape. He cut the
hole through the picketing and headed the desperate charge, which
was opposed by a thick line of savages who, anticipating some such
attempt, had placed themselves in position along a fence for the
purpose of making escape impossible. It is indeed a marvel that
anybody should have succeeded in breaking through their line and
reaching the woods beyond. Dr. Holmes had his clothes riddled
with bullets as he ran, but he managed to reach the thick woods
unhurt, and there concealed himself in the hole made by the up-
rooting of a large tree. Remaining thus hidden until night, he was
not discovered by any of the bands of Indians who beat the bushes
in every direction, bent upon leaving no white man or friendly
Indian alive. After night he had intended to make his escape under cover of darkness from the neighbourhood, but the light from
burning buildings prevented this until midnight, when, by careful
creeping, he made his way without discovery, among the camp-
fires of the sleeping savages, who now rested from their bloody toil.
As Dr. Holmes could not swim, it was impossible for him to cross
the river to the forts and settlements there, and hence he wandered
about in the swamp for five days, living upon roots and other such
things, until finally, almost famished, he emerged from the cane-
brakes and sought the highlands, really caring very little in his desperation whether he should fall into the hands of friends or foes.
Coming upon some horses which were tied, and finding that they
belonged to white men who were somewhere near, he fired his
gun to attract their attention; but unluckily it alarmed them, and

they fled to the river and hid themselves, remaining there for two days and nights. Left thus alone, Holmes went to a house in the neighbourhood, and succeeded in catching some chickens, which in his ravenous hunger he ate raw. He was finally discovered by a white man, the owner of the place, and taken to a place of safety. Many years afterward he related the story of his adventures to Mr. Pickett, from whose pages we have condensed it.

Lieutenant Chambliss was twice severely wounded in his flight, but reached the friendly woods at last and concealed himself in a heap of logs, meaning to make his way to a place of safety as soon as night should fall. About dark, however, a roving band of the savages surrounded the log heap, and to the dismay of poor Chambliss, set fire to it. His position was terrible. The fire rapidly ate into the pile, and to remain there was to be roasted alive, while any attempt to come out would be met, of course, by immediate destruction with knife or tomahawk. The fire was now scorching him, but he lay still, enduring it as long as it was possible to suffer in silence. Just as it became absolutely necessary for him to withdraw, he was delighted to see the Indians, who had now lighted their pipes, walking away. Silently, in order that the savages might not hear him, he crept out of the burning pile and concealed himself more effectually elsewhere. Wounded and famishing he wandered about for awhile, managing at last to reach Mount Vernon.

The most romantic incident of this terrible affair remains to be told. Zachariah McGirth, with his half-breed wife and his children, was one of the inmates of Fort Mims until the day of the massacre. On the morning of that day, a few hours before the attack was made, he left the fort, intending to visit his plantation at a point higher up on the Alabama River. Leaving his family in the fort he went to the river, accompanied by some negroes, and began his journey in a boat. He had gone but a few miles when the sound of the firing at the fort reached his ears, and he thus learned that the attack had come. Anxious about the fate of his wife and children, he turned back, and secreting himself in the woods, passed the long afternoon in a state of the most terrible suspense. When the sound of musketry at last died away, the great volumes of smoke revealed to him the fact—horrible in its significance to him—that the savages had triumphed. Desperate now with distress, he hid the negroes and boldly went to the scene of the slaughter, not caring whether the Indians had left or not. Finding no savages there, but seeing heaps of the slain everywhere, he summoned his negroes and began a search for the bodies of his wife and children. They were nowhere to be found, and McGirth was forced to conclude that his family were among those who had been burned in the buildings.

As a matter of fact, McGirth's wife and children were the half-breed family who had been spared, as related in the preceding chapter. There was a young warrior among Weatherford's men who, many years before, when he was an orphan and hungry, had been tenderly cared for by McGirth's wife, and during the horrible slaughter at Fort Mims this young warrior happened to recognize the woman who had befriended him in his time of sorest need. To save her and her children he had to tell his comrades that he wished to make them his slaves, and under this pretence he carried them to his home in the nation.

McGirth knew nothing of this, of course, and as he had very tenderly loved his family, he now became entirely reckless of danger, not caring to live, but being desperately bent upon doing all that he could for the destruction of the Creeks, who, as he believed, had bereft him of his wife and his children. He became the most daring scout and express rider in the American service, making the most perilous journeys, shrinking from no danger, and many times serving the American cause when nobody else could be found to perform the important duties which he undertook. One day, several months after the massacre at Fort Mims, McGirth was in Mobile, when some one came to him with a message, saying that a party of poor Indians who had made their way down the river from the hostile country wished to see him. Answering the summons he was ushered into the presence of his wife and seven children, whom he had thought of for months, as among the victims of the savages at Fort Mims. It was as if they had suddenly arisen from the dead.

CHAPTER 12

The Dog Charge

It was a part of Weatherford's tactics to prevent the concentration of his enemies as far as that was possible, and to keep the whole country round about in such a state of apprehension that no troops or militiamen could be spared from one stockade fort for the assistance of another. Accordingly, when he advanced to the assault on Fort Mims he sent the prophet Francis with a force of Creeks into the country which lies in the fork of the Alabama and Tombigbee rivers, and which in our day constitutes Clarke County. In this part of the country there were several stockade forts erected, one in each neighbourhood, by the settlers, as a precautionary measure, when the disturbed state of the country first aroused serious apprehensions. Fort Sinquefield, named, as all these fortresses were, after the owner of the place on which it was built, stood a few miles north-east of the village of Grove Hill, which is now the county seat of Clarke County. Fort White was further to the west, and Fort Glass was about fifteen miles to the south, near the spot on which the present village of Suggsville stands.

When the battle of Burnt Corn brought actual war into being, most of the settlers removed with their families into these forts and prepared to defend themselves. When General Claiborne arrived with his seven hundred men he sent some small reinforcements to these posts, under command of Colonel Carson, who rebuilding Fort Glass, christened it Fort Madison, and made it his head-quarters and the head-quarters of the district round about.

It was the mission of the prophet Francis to harass this part of the country, and on the next day but one after the massacre at

Fort Mims, Francis struck his first blow within two miles of Fort Sinquefield. Notwithstanding the general alarm, Abner James and Ransom Kimball, with their families, numbering seventeen souls in all, remained at Kimball's house, intending within a day or two to remove to the fort. Francis attacked the house and killed twelve of the seventeen persons. The other five escaped in various ways. One of those who escaped was Isham Kimball, a youth sixteen years of age, who survived the war, became a public officer in his county, and was living there as late as the year 1857; from his account and that of Mrs. Merrill, a married daughter of Abner James, who also was living in Clarke County in 1857, the original recorders of this bit of history derived their information with respect to details.

Mrs. Merrill's adventures were very strange and romantic, and as we shall not again have occasion to write of her, it may not be amiss to interrupt the regular course of this narrative and tell what happened to her. At the time of the massacre at Kimball's house, she, with her infant child in her arms, was knocked down, scalped, and left as one dead among the slain. She lay senseless for many hours, but during the night she revived, and with a mother's instinct began to search among the dead bodies of her kinsmen for her babe. She was overjoyed to find that it still breathed, although some member of the savage band had made an effort to scalp it, cutting its head all round, but failing—probably because the hair was so short—to finish the horrible operation. The poor mother, well-nigh dead though she was, made haste to give her babe the breast, and had the gratification of seeing it revive rapidly in consequence. Then, taking it in her arms, she made an effort to reach Fort Sinquefield, about two miles distant. Finding at last that her strength was failing rapidly, and that she could carry the child no longer, she secreted it and used the little remaining strength she had in crawling to the stockade and entreating some one there to rescue her child. This of course was quickly done, and notwithstanding the severity of her injuries both she and the child recovered under good treatment.

But the strangest, or at any rate the most romantic, part of the story is yet to be told. At the time of these occurrences Mrs. Merrill's husband was absent, serving as a volunteer under General Claiborne. The news of the butchery, including the positive information that Mrs. Merrill and her child were slain, was carried to the post where Merrill was serving, and he heard nothing of her wonderful escape. During one of the battles which followed each other rapidly that autumn, Merrill, before his anxious wife found any means of communicating with him, was terribly wounded and left for dead on the battle-field, and the report of his death was borne to his wife. Recovering his consciousness after his comrades had left the field, Merrill fell in with some Tennessee volunteers, and was sent with their wounded to Tennessee, where, after long nursing, he was finally restored to health. After several years had passed Mrs. Merrill married again, without even a suspicion that her first husband was living—believing indeed that she knew him to be dead. She was living happily with her second husband and with a large family growing up about her, when one evening a family who were emigrating from Tennessee to Texas stopped at her house and asked for entertainment for a night. They were hospitably received after the generous custom of the time and country, but they had scarcely settled themselves as guests before the head of the emigrating family and the wife of the host recognized each other. The one was Merrill and the other was his wife, and both had married again, each believing the other to be dead. After some consultation it was decided that, as each had acted in perfectly good faith, and as both the families were happy as they were, it would be the part of wisdom to let matters stand, and to live their new lives without trying to recover the old.

Let us now return to the regular order of events. When the tidings of the massacre at Kimball's house reached Fort Madison, Colonel Carson sent a detachment of ten men to the spot, and they at once carried the bodies of the dead persons to Fort Sinquefield for burial. On the third of September the whole body of people in Fort Sinquefield, with that inexplicable carelessness which so often marked the conduct of the whites at this time, left the fort, unarmed, and went out to a valley some fifty yards away, to attend the burial services over the bodies of their friends. The wily prophet was awaiting precisely such an opportunity as this, and while the men were filling the grave, he charged over a neighbouring hill, and tried to put his force between the un-armed garrison and the gate of the fort. Luckily he had somewhat further to run than the fort people had, and so the men of the place managed to gain the gate; but, alas! the women and children were nearly all outside, and Francis's warriors were between them and the entrance to the fort. Their plight appeared to be a hopeless one, and it would have been so but for the courage and the presence of mind of one young man, whose name is given by Mr. Pickett as Isaac Heaton, but who is called Isaac Haden by Mr. A. B. Meek, a very careful writer, and one particularly well informed about this part of the field. The latter name is adopted here, as probably the correct one. This young man Haden was fond of field sports, and kept a large pack of hounds, trained to chase and seize any living thing upon which their master might set them. At the critical moment, young Haden, mounted upon a good horse and accompanied by his sixty dogs, arrived at the gate from a cattle driving expedition. In an instant he saw the situation of affairs, and with a promptitude which showed remarkable presence of mind, he resolved upon a daring attempt to rescue the women and children. With the whoop of the huntsman this gallant fellow set spurs to his horse, and charged the Indians with his trained pack of ferocious hounds. The suddenness of the onset and the novelty of the attack threw the savages into complete confusion. The fierce dogs seized the naked savages and tore them furiously, and for several minutes their attention was entirely absorbed in an effort to beat the brutes off. Meanwhile the men of the fort reinforced the dogs with all their might, and thus a road was kept open for the retreat of the women and children, every one of whom, except a Mrs. Phillips, who was killed and scalped, escaped within the gates. Young Haden narrowly escaped death as the price of his heroism—for it was heroism of the highest sort. His horse was killed under him, and when he was at last safe within the fort, it was found that five bullets had passed through his clothes, but the brave fellow was not hurt.

Francis speedily recovered from his temporary perplexity, and rallying his men he made a furious assault upon the fort; but the gates were now shut, and the resolute men behind the pickets were skilled marksmen, who delivered their fire with deadly precision.

THE DOG CHARGE AT FORT SINQUIFIELD

The savages were repulsed and the fort's company for the time saved, with the loss of but one man and one boy, who, with Mrs. Phillips killed outside the gates, made the total number of the slain in this assault only three persons.

The wiser members of the fort's company perceived, however, that the place was not strong enough to be successfully defended against a really determined attack by an adequate force; and accordingly, after some discussion it was resolved to evacuate the place and retire to Fort Madison, before the second and more determined attack, which Francis was sure to make, should render it too late. That night the whole company of Sinquefield silently withdrew, and after a perilous march of fifteen miles through a country infested with savages, reached their destination in safety.

About this time four men went from Fort Madison to some fields in the neighbourhood for supplies of green vegetables, and while gathering these they were attacked and two of them were shot. Colonel Carson having satisfied himself that the peninsula which he was set to guard was full of Indians, and believing that Red Eagle with the victors of Fort Mims would direct his next blow at Fort Madison, resolved to call upon General Claiborne, who was now at Fort Stoddard, for assistance. A particularly bold young man, of whom we shall hear more after a while, by name Jeremiah Austill—or Jerry Austill, as he was always called—volunteered to undertake the dangerous duty of carrying Colonel Carson's despatch. Mounting his horse about nightfall, he said goodbye to friends who had little hope of seeing him again, and rode away. After an all night's journey the brave young fellow arrived at General Claiborne's head-quarters, and told the general whence he had come, greatly to the surprise and admiration of that officer, who highly commended his courage and devotion to the common cause.

General Claiborne was in great perplexity, however. The Fort Mims massacre and the rapidly following depredations in other directions had produced a genuine panic among the settlers who now poured into the forts, crowding them to overflowing; and in the state of alarm which prevailed everywhere, the commanders of all the forts were convinced that their fighting forces were insufficient to defend the posts entrusted to their charge. When

young Austill arrived, therefore, with Colonel Carson's application for reinforcements, it was only one of a dozen or a score of
similar demands, and with the meagre force at his disposal General Claiborne was wholly unable to satisfy the requirements of his
subordinates. In his perplexity he saw but one method of solving
the problem, and that was to order the evacuation of some of the
forts and the concentration of the fighting men at fewer points.
To this course there was the serious objection, that the stockade posts were already inconveniently and unwholesomely over-
crowded, and a good deal of sickness existed as a consequence;
but there was no other way of meeting the exigencies of the
situation. General Claiborne therefore sent young Austill back
to Fort Madison with a message which has been variously represented in different accounts of the affair. It appears, however, from
General Claiborne's manuscripts, that the message, as it was given
to Austill, was to the effect that as there were no troops to spare
for the reinforcement of Fort Madison, and as St. Stephen's was
strategically a more important post, Colonel Carson should evacuate Fort Madison and retire with his garrison and the inmates of
his fort to St. Stephen's, if in his judgment that course was wisest
in the circumstances. In other words, General Claiborne wished
Colonel Carson to use his discretion, after learning that no troops
could be sent to his assistance; but either because the message was
ambiguous in itself, or because young Austill delivered it inaccu-
rately, Colonel Carson understood that he was peremptorily ordered to evacuate his fort, and the order as thus understood gave
great dissatisfaction to everybody concerned. The people loudly
complained that General Claiborne was abandoning their part of
the country to its fate. Colonel Carson, of course, had no choice
but to obey the order as he understood it, but those of the settlers
who were not regularly enlisted soldiers were free to do as they
pleased, and under the lead of Captain Evan Austill, the father of
Jeremiah Austill, and himself a very resolute man, fifty men of the
neighbourhood according to one account, eighty according to
another, with their families, determined to remain at Fort Madison. All the rest of the people in the fort, about four hundred in
number, marched to St. Stephen's. The little band who remained
were very vigilant, and managed to protect themselves effectu-

ally, until after a time Colonel Carson was instructed to return and regarrison the fort. Colonel Carson had scarcely reached St. Stephen's, indeed, before a second despatch came from General Claiborne, speaking of the former message as discretionary, and urging Carson not to abandon the fort "unless it is clear that you cannot hold it." Among the gallant little company who remained at Fort Madison was Sam Dale, who, it will be remembered, led the advance at Burnt Corn, and whom we shall see again.

CHAPTER 13

Pushmatahaw and His Warriors

There was great anxiety felt from the beginning of the war lest the Creeks should succeed in drawing the Chickasaws and Choctaws into the conflict as allies. At that stage of affairs at which we have now arrived this fear had become a very nightmare. The few troops at Claiborne's command, together with the militia of the country, were barely sufficient to hold the forts, and even this inadequate force was liable at any time to be reduced by the withdrawal of the soldiers to assist in repelling an attack of the British, whose fleet now constantly threatened the coast; and if the forces of the Choctaws and Chickasaws should be added to Red Eagle's strength, the plight of the whites would indeed be pitiable.

About this time a Choctaw chief of influence with his people, by name Pushmatahaw, arrived at St. Stephen's, and declared that he could induce a considerable number of the Choctaw warriors to enlist in the American service, if permission were given to him to recruit among them. Eagerly grasping at this hope, Colonel George S. Gaines[1] went with the chief to Mobile to secure the desired authority from General Flournoy, who was now in command of the South-western Department.

That officer, for some reason which is not apparent, declined to accept the proffered services of the Choctaws, and Colonel Gaines and his companion returned with heavy hearts to St. Stephen's, where the news they brought created the profoundest dissatisfaction. Before the friendly chief had taken his departure,

1: Colonel Gaines was still living in the year 1866 at State Line, Mississippi. The author met him in that year engaged, old and feeble as he was, in a charitable work that involved considerable labour.

however, a courier from General Flournoy arrived, bringing an order which directed Colonel Gaines to accept the chief's offer of assistance, and to accompany him to the Choctaw Nation to enlist the men.

With a single white companion Colonel Gaines went with Pushmatahaw to the nation, where, gathering the Choctaws into a council, the chief made them a speech, saying that Tecumseh, who had suggested this war, was a bad man. He added:

> He came through our country, but did not turn our heads. He went among the Muscogees, and got many of them to join him. You know the Tensaw people. They were our friends. They played ball with us. They sheltered and fed us when we went to Pensacola. Where are they now? Their bodies are rotting at Sam Mims's place. The people at St. Stephen's are also our friends. The Muscogees intend to kill them too. They want soldiers to defend them. You can all do as you please. You are free men. I dictate to none of you; but I shall join the St. Stephen's people. If you have a mind to follow me, I will lead you to glory and to victory.

Pushmatahaw finished this speech with his drawn sword in his hand. When he paused, one of the hitherto silent warriors stood up and, striking his breast with his open palm, after the manner of the Choctaws on specially solemn occasions, said, "I am a man; I will follow you;" whereupon his fellows imitated his example, and thus a considerable force of men, who might have been added to Weatherford's strength but for the friendliness of Pushmatahaw, became active friends of the whites.

But a new factor of very much greater value was now about to enter into the problem and totally change its conditions. Andrew Jackson, the sternest and most energetic of Indian fighters, was coming with his Tennessee volunteers to reverse the situation of affairs. The Creeks, who were now hunting the whites like wild beasts, were presently to become the hunted party, with Andrew Jackson upon their track.

CHAPTER 14

Jackson is Helped Into His Saddle

Bad news travels rapidly, and the news of the terrible massacre at Fort Mims was soon known in all parts of the South and West. There were neither railroads nor steamboats in those days, and between the Tensaw settlement and the rest of the country there were not even stage-coaches running, or mail-riders on horseback. It took more than a month for the swiftest messenger from Southern Alabama to reach New York, and nearly as long to reach Washington City; but when Red Eagle had shown of what mettle he was made, General Claiborne, who in his double capacity as Governor of Louisiana and general in the field was doubly interested, became greatly alarmed, and that with good reason. The British were threatening the coast, and Weatherford now appeared to threaten Mobile. The situation was, indeed, an alarming one. It was pretty clear that Weatherford was already acting in concert, more or less direct, with the enemy without; and if he should take the town of Mobile, as he was probably able to do, securing a base of operations for a British force, he might easily turn back and utterly destroy the settlements, while the few troops within reach should be engaged with the British.

In this perilous situation of affairs it was useless for General Claiborne, or his superior officer, General Flournoy, to appeal to the government at Washington for aid. Even if the troops of the Government had not been fully occupied already in other parts of the country, the distance was so great that any assistance which the general government might be able to render must of necessity come too late to be of any avail. It would take a month for the messenger asking for help to reach Washington, another month for a force to be gathered, and perhaps two months more for it to reach the exposed point. Three or four months at least, and probably a greater time, must pass before help could come from that quarter, and it might as well have taken a hundred years, so far as all practical purposes were concerned.

The only resource, therefore, was an appeal to the people of the surrounding States. Messengers were sent in hot haste to South Carolina, Georgia, and Tennessee, carrying despatches which simply set forth the facts and the danger, and asked for help. The response was quick and generous. Georgians and South Carolinians began at once to organize forces, which soon afterward invaded the Creek country. But the most efficient aid was to come from Tennessee, a State which had already shown itself quick to answer to every demand made upon it. It had furnished its full quotas of men to the national army; and less than a year before the time of which we now write, it had sent a full division of volunteers under Jackson to reinforce the army at New Orleans. This division had been ordered to disband while at Natchez, when they were without money or provisions with which to reach their homes, but Jackson had resolutely disobeyed the order, and instead of disbanding his division had marched it back to Tennessee in a body.

There had been loud murmurs at the treatment these volunteers had received, but when the news came that the people of the Tensaw country were suffering brutal butchery at the hands of savages, and that Mobile was threatened, Tennessee hushed her murmurs, and promptly responded to the call.

On the 18th day of September, the people of Nashville assembled in a public meeting to consider the news which had just been received. General Jackson lay upon his bed, weak, emaciated, and racked with pain from a wound received in a street fight; but everybody felt that his counsel in matters of this kind was essential. Indeed, it was known that upon the question of his ability to lead the forces that were to be raised their success in raising forces at all must in a great measure depend. The meeting, therefore, did no business on the first day, except to express its members' determination to render assistance to their brethren in the South, and to appoint a committee, headed by Colonel (afterward General) Coffee, to consult with the Governor of the State and with General Jackson, and to report the result.

81

This committee went to Jackson's chamber and told him the story of Fort Mims, and of the need there was for him to lead the Tennessee volunteers. They assured him also that if they could give his name to the people as the leader who would head them, the volunteers would flock to the standard of the State at once.

Jackson replied that he was recovering, although he was still confined to his bed, and that he thought he should be well enough to mount his horse by the time the troops could be got ready to march. In that event he promised to take command.

With this news the committee went to the clergyman who was chairman of the public meeting, and that patriotic man, dismissing all thought of his regular church services, called the meeting together again the next morning, which happened to be Sunday. The voice of the meeting and of the people of the State was unanimous. Mr. Parton, in his Life of Andrew Jackson, writes:

> The news of the massacre produced everywhere in Tennessee the most profound impression. Pity for the distressed Alabamians, fears for the safety of their own borders, rage against the Creeks, so long the recipients of the governmental bounty, united to inflame the minds of the people. But one feeling pervaded the state. With one vow it was decreed that the entire resources and the whole available force of Tennessee should be hurled upon the savage foe, to avenge the massacre and deliver the southern country.

There was unfortunately no law of the State under which anybody was authorized to call out the needed men, and although Governor Blount was ready to approve and actively to encourage the gathering of Tennessee's strength and its use in this way, he had no legal authority to promise pay or support to the troops. This defect was repaired by the Legislature within a week. That body passed a bill authorizing the Governor to enlist three thousand five hundred men for this service, voting three hundred thousand dollars for expenses, and pledging the State to support and pay the men, if the general government should refuse or neglect to accept the force as a part of its volunteer army.

Meantime, from his sick bed, and without waiting for the processes of law, General Jackson called for volunteers. He published an address, in which he said to his Tennesseeans:

The horrid butcheries perpetrating on our defenceless fellow-citizens near Fort Stoddard cannot fail to excite in every bosom a spirit of revenge. The subjoined letter of our worthy Governor shows that the general government has deposited no authority in this quarter to afford aid to the unhappy sufferers. It is wished that volunteers should go forward, relying on the justice of the general government for ultimate remuneration. It surely never would be said that the brave Tennesseeans wanted other inducements than patriotism and humanity to rush to the aid of our bleeding neighbours, their friends and relations. I feel confident that the dull calculations of sneaking prudence will not prevent you from immediately stepping forth on this occasion, so worthy the arm of every brave soldier and good citizen. I regret that indisposition, which from present appearances is not likely to continue long, may prevent me from leading the van; but indulge the grateful hope of sharing with you the dangers and glory of prostrating these hell-hounds, who are capable of such barbarities.

Jackson was in a hurry. Every day at such a time was precious, and hence he was determined to waste no time coddling his worn and wounded body. He issued his addresses and his orders from his sick-bed; concerted measures with General John Cocke, who was to command the troops from the eastern half of the State, and made arrangements for provisions. On the 26th day of September, just one week after the Sunday when the public meeting had been held, he sent Coffee forward with the advance of his army a body of horsemen numbering somewhat more than five hundred. Coffee received volunteers at every cross-road, and by the time he arrived at Fayetteville, Alabama, the appointed place of rendezvous, his five hundred men had increased to one thousand three hundred.

Jackson had to be helped on his horse when he set out to join the army he had raised so speedily. His arm was still encased in the surgeon's wrappings, and carried in a sling. He could put but one arm into his coat-sleeve, and he was so weak that it was with difficulty that he could ride at all; but there was that in his composition which had already gained for him his nickname, "Old Hickory;" it was the tough hickory of his nature which supplied the place of physical strength, and enabled him to march. Everywhere he issued his proclamations and addresses, couched in strong, vigorous, though not always graceful, English: a practice for which he has been laughed at sometimes, but one which was wise, nevertheless. He knew his Tennesseeans, and adapted his measures to their character. They were an impulsive race of men, full of warm blood, which was easily stirred by such appeals as Jackson made to them, though they would not have been moved by a colder species of address.

Having secured his men, Jackson's next care was to convert them as rapidly as possible into soldiers, and accordingly his next appeal was directed to this end. Finding that he would not be able to reach Fayetteville at the exact time appointed for the rendezvous, he sent an officer forward with the following address, which was read to the troops:

We are about to furnish these savages a lesson of admonition. We are about to teach them that our long forbearance has not proceeded from an insensibility to wrongs or an inability to redress them. They stand in need of such warning. In proportion as we have borne with their insults and submitted to their outrages, they have multiplied in number and increased in atrocity. But the measure of their offences is at length filled. The blood of our women and children recently spilt at Fort Mims calls for our vengeance; it must not call in vain. Our borders must no longer be disturbed by the war-whoop of these savages and the cries of their suffering victims. The torch that has been lighted up must be made to blaze in the heart of their own country. It is time they should be made to feel the weight of a power which, because it was merciful, they believed to be impotent. But how shall a war so long forborne, and so loudly called for by retributive justice, be waged? Shall we imitate the example of our enemies in the disorder of their movements and the savageness of their dispositions? Is it worth the character of American soldiers, who take up arms to redress the wrongs of our injured country, to assume no better models than those furnished them by barbarians? No, fellow-soldiers, great as are the grievances that have called us from our homes, we must not permit disorderly passions to tarnish the reputation we shall carry along with us. We must and will be victorious; but we must conquer as men who owe nothing to chance, and who in the midst of victory can still be mindful of what is due to humanity! We will commence the campaign by an inviolable attention to discipline and subordination. Without a strict observance of these, victory must ever be uncertain, and ought hardly to be exulted in even when gained. To what but the entire disregard of order and subordination are we to ascribe the disasters which have attended our arms in the north during the present war? How glorious will it be to remove the blots which have tarnished the fair character bequeathed us by the fathers of our Revolution! The bosom of your general is full of hope. He knows the ardour which animates you, and already exults in the triumph which your strict observance of discipline and good order will render certain.

CHAPTER 15

The March to Enemy Country

Coffee had pushed on with his cavalry brigade to Huntsville, Alabama, thirty-two miles beyond Fayetteville, without waiting for Jackson. At Fayetteville, Jackson found the army to whom he had issued his proclamation, but their numbers were much smaller than he had hoped—not exceeding a thousand men; and it would have been necessary, probably, to wait for recruits to come in, if there had been no other cause for waiting. Every thing had to be done, and day and night Jackson was busy with details pertaining to the organization, the drilling, and the disciplining of the troops; for this volunteer general knew, as few volunteers do, how greatly discipline and drill increase the strength of an armed force.

Luckily he had time for this, somewhat unexpectedly. He had supposed that the victorious Creeks would march upon Mobile, and his haste was largely due to his anxiety to attack them in rear, and thus save the important seaport and prevent a junction of the Creeks with the British. Soon after his arrival at Fayetteville, however, which was on the 7th of October, Jackson received a despatch from General Coffee, saying that instead of marching upon Mobile the Creeks were moving northward in two columns, threatening Georgia and Tennessee.

Why Red Eagle pursued this course was long a puzzle to students of the campaign. He was so manifestly a man of quick and accurate perceptions in military matters, that he must have seen how entirely Mobile was within his grasp, and how great an advantage it would be to him to capture or destroy the town; and when he neglected such an opportunity it was not easy to guess why he did so. The mystery was solved when a letter was found in his own house a month or so later, dated September 29th, 1813, from Manxique, the Spanish Governor of Florida. This letter was addressed to the chiefs of the Creek nation, and was in these words:

Gentlemen:

I received the letter that you wrote me in the month of August, by which, and with great satisfaction, I was informed of the advantages which your brave warriors obtained over your enemies. I represented, as I promised you, to the Captain-General of the Havana, the request which, the last time I took you by the hand, you made me of arms and ammunitions; but until now I cannot yet have an answer. But I am in hopes that he will send me the effects which I requested, and as soon as I receive them I shall inform you. I am very thankful for your generous offers to procure to me the provisions and warriors necessary in order to retake the port of Mobile, and you ask me at the same time if we have given up Mobile to the Americans: to which I answer, for the present I cannot profit of your generous offer, not being at war with the Americans, who did not take Mobile by force, since they purchased it from the miserable officer, destitute of honour, who commanded there, and delivered it without authority. By which reasons the sale and delivery of that place is entirely void and null, and I hope that the Americans will restore it again to us, because nobody can dispose of thing that is not his own property; in consequence of which the Spaniards have not lost their right to it. And I hope you will not put in execution the project you tell me of, to burn the town, since these houses and properties do not belong to the Americans, but to true Spaniards. To the bearers of your letter I have ordered some small presents to be given, and I remain forever your good father and friend,

Manxique

It is a pleasure to reflect, that about a year later, Jackson, acting on his own responsibility, marched to Pensacola and humiliated the successor of this especial rascal, who wrote about honour in a letter in which he was encouraging and planning to furnish arms and ammunition to savages who were butchering the people of a nation with whom his own country was at peace. The letter explains Weatherford's course. He was acting from the first in concert with this Spanish governor, from whom he was drawing his arms and ammunition; and while he wanted to burn Mobile, he knew that he must first ask Manxique's permission. Accordingly, he must have sent a letter to that ally on the very day of the massacre at Fort Mims, or on the next day at latest. That massacre began at noon and ended at five o'clock on the 30th day of August; and Manxique speaks of the letter reporting the victory as "the letter that you wrote me in the month of August." It is thus clear that Weatherford's military instincts were neither asleep nor at fault when he finished that bloody day's work; that he saw both the possibility and the advantage of destroying Mobile, and at once asked permission to do so. The letter denying that permission to him was dated September 29th; and, as he was marching upon Tennessee and Georgia early in October, it is apparent that he had only waited for the arrival of the Spanish governor's reply, before renewing his campaign. While he hoped for permission to destroy the seaport town, he waited; the moment he knew that he must not do that, he began his northward and eastward march, to strike his enemies in another quarter. His failure to march upon Mobile has been cited by some writers to prove that Weatherford was after all only an Indian, without real military capacity; in the light of all the facts, as they are revealed by the letter quoted, his proceedings prove precisely the reverse. We are indebted for the sparing of Mobile, not to incompetency on Weatherford's part, but to the greed of the Spaniard, who hesitated to permit the destruction of property which he hoped to get possession of by other means.

When Coffee's report of the advance of the Creeks came, the news greatly relieved Jackson of anxiety. It freed him from apprehension concerning Mobile; it promised to save him from a long and wearying march through a wilderness, and to enable him to meet the enemy sooner than would otherwise have been possible; and his chief desire now was to hurl his army with crushing force against the Creeks, to make unceasing war upon them, and to break their power as speedily as possible. He was so elated at the prospect of an early encounter with them, that he wrote in a playful vein to Coffee, saying:

It is surely high gratification to learn that the Creeks are so attentive to my situation as to save me the pain of travelling. I must not be outdone in politeness, and will therefore endeavour to meet them on middle ground.[1]

A good deal remained to be done, and arrangements were not yet complete for the procuring of provisions. Coffee was at Huntsville, and was watching for the enemy. On the 11th of October, Coffee reported the Indian advance, and Jackson marched on the instant, arriving at Huntsville that evening. At Huntsville it was necessary to await the arrival of provisions for the army. Supplies from East Tennessee had been sent down the river, but a failure of water in the shallow stream detained them on the way. Jackson marched to Ditto's landing to await their coming; but they came not, and relief seemed to be impossible. Jackson was in a sore strait. He wanted to advance, but was without provisions or an immediate prospect of getting any. He ordered Coffee with his cavalry to scour the Indian country for supplies, while with the main army he made a toilsome march, over a mountainous country, to Thompson's Creek, about twenty miles higher up the river, for the double purpose of meeting the expected provisions there, and of putting himself in the way of marching the more quickly to the relief of a body of friendly Indians who occupied a fort at the Ten Islands, on the Coosa River.

Meantime, Jackson sent messengers in every direction, urging everybody in any sort of authority to hurry the supplies forward. At Thompson's Creek he built a fort, as a base of supplies for the campaign. His plight was desperate, but he would not stay where he was or fall back. With food or without it, he meant to march into the Indian country and dare starvation as he braved the other perils of war. It is related of him that at one time during the campaign, when the men were without provisions, one of them saw him eating something, and mutinously demanded a share of the food.

"Certainly," replied Jackson, thrusting his hand into his pocket and offering the man some acorns. He was literally living on acorns while marching and fighting night and day.

The state of affairs when Jackson was about leaving Fort Deposit, on Thompson's Creek, where he tarried but a single day, may

1: Parton's *Life of Jackson.*

be inferred from a letter written by Major John Reid, of the general's staff, from which we copy some passages. The whole letter is printed in Parton's Life of Jackson.

> At this place we have remained a day for the purpose of establishing a depot for provisions; but where these provisions are to come from God Almighty only knows. We had expected supplies from East Tennessee, but they have not arrived, and I am fearful never will. I speak seriously when I declare I expect we shall soon have to eat our horses, and perhaps this is the best use we can put a great many of them to.
>
> The hostile Creeks, as we learnt yesterday from the Path Killer, are assembling in great numbers within fifteen miles from Turkey Town. Chenully, who is posted with the friendly Creeks in the neighbourhood of that place, it is feared will be destroyed before we can arrive to their relief. In three days we shall probably have a fight. The general swears he will neither sound a retreat nor survive a defeat.... We shall leave this place with less than two days' provisions.

It seems almost incredible that a general should venture to advance into an enemy's country, beginning the march with only provisions enough to last his force for a day or two, and with no assurance, scarcely even a hope, that provisions were likely to follow him; but this is what Jackson did.

Coffee joined him on the march, bringing with him a few hundreds of bushels of corn, and reporting that he had destroyed some Indian towns, but had encountered none of the Indians. The corn was a mere handful among the men and horses of the army, but cries for help were coming every hour from the friendly Indians, whose situation at the Ten Islands was desperate, and Jackson marched forward, trusting to chance for supplies. He meant to fight first and find something to eat afterward.

As has been said, the army remained but one day at Fort Deposit, and during that day constructed a fortress; but Jackson found time in which to write an address to his men, whom he was now about to lead upon a campaign in which they would encounter famine and hardships of the sorest kind, as well as the savage enemy. They needed all the courage that enthusiasm in the cause could give them, and the address was designed to key them up, so to speak, to the pitch of their commander's temper. The address read as follows:

You have, fellow-soldiers, at length penetrated the country of your enemies. It is not to be believed that they will abandon the soil that embosoms the bones of their forefathers without furnishing you an opportunity of signalizing your valour. Wise men do not expect, brave men will not desire it. It was not to travel unmolested through a barren wilderness that you quitted your families and homes, and submitted to so many privations: it was to revenge the cruelties committed upon your defenceless frontiers by the inhuman Creeks, instigated by their no less inhuman allies; you shall not be disappointed.

If the enemy flee before us we will overtake and chastise him; we will teach him how dreadful, when once aroused, is the resentment of freemen. But it is not by boasting that punishment is to be inflicted or victory obtained. The same resolution that prompted us to take up arms must inspire us in battle. Men thus animated and thus resolved, barbarians can never conquer; and it is an enemy barbarous in the extreme that we have now to face. Their reliance will be on the damage they can do you while you are asleep and unprepared for action; their hopes shall fail them in the hour of experiment. Soldiers who know their duty and are ambitious to perform it are not to be taken by surprise. Our sentinels will never sleep, nor our soldiers be unprepared for action; yet while it is enjoined upon the sentinels vigilantly to watch the approach of the foe, they are at the same time commanded not to fire at shadows. Imaginary dangers must not deprive them of entire self-possession. Our soldiers will lie with their arms in their hands; and the moment an alarm is given they will move to their respective positions without noise and without confusion. They will thus be enabled to hear the orders of their officers, and to obey them with promptitude.

Great reliance will be placed by the enemy, on the consternation they may be able to spread through our ranks by the hideous yells with which they commence their battles;

but brave men will laugh at such efforts to alarm them. It is not by bellowings and screams that the wounds of death are inflicted. You will teach these noisy assailants how weak are their weapons of warfare, by opposing them with the bayonet. What Indian ever withstood its charge? What army of any nation ever withstood it long?

Yes, soldiers, the order for a charge will be the signal for victory. In that moment your enemy will be seen flying in every direction before you. But in the moment of action coolness and deliberation must be regarded; your fire made with precision and aim; and when ordered to charge with the bayonet you must proceed to the assault with a quick and firm step, without trepidation or alarm. Then shall you behold the completion of your hopes, in the discomfiture of your enemy. Your general, whose duty as well as inclination is to watch over your safety, will not, to gratify any wishes of his own, rush you unnecessarily into danger. He knows, however, that it is not in assailing an enemy that men are destroyed; it is when retreating and in confusion. Aware of this, he will be prompted as much by a regard for your lives as your honour. He laments that he has been compelled, even incidentally, to hint at a retreat when speaking to freemen and to soldiers. Never until you forget all that is due to yourselves and your country will you have any practical understanding of that word. Shall an enemy wholly unacquainted with military evolutions, and who rely more for victory on their grim visages and hideous yells than upon their bravery or their weapons—shall such an enemy ever drive before them the well-trained youths of our country, whose bosoms pant for glory, and a desire to avenge the wrongs they have received? Your general will not live to behold such a spectacle; rather would he rush into the thickest of the enemy and submit himself to their scalping-knives. But he has no fears of such a result. He knows the valour of the men he commands, and how certainly that valour, regulated as it will be, will lead to victory. With his soldiers he will face all dangers, and with them participate in the glory of conquest.

Nothing could have been better fitted than this address was to serve the end for which it was designed. Jackson knew his Tennesseeans, both in their temper and in their habits; and he adroitly managed to warn them against the consequences of those faults which were most prominent in their characters, while seeming merely to appeal in a stimulating fashion to their pride of courage. He knew, as they did not, how trying the hardships of a campaign in a wilderness with insufficient supplies are; he knew how prone raw troops are to fall into confusion and panic in the excitement of a sudden attack; and against all these things he did what could be done to brace them by an adroit appeal to their pride of race and of personal courage. If some of his expressions seem to suggest any thing like contempt of the Creeks as foes, they were meant merely to arouse the pride of his own men, and indicated no disposition on his part not to "respect his enemy," as Claiborne said. On the contrary, he showed the profoundest respect for his enemy by his extreme solicitude about the condition and the conduct of his own men.

The marching was now as nearly continuous as was possible in the circumstances. Frequent pauses had to be made, in order that provisions might be gathered from the surrounding country, but as soon as there was food in camp the march was resumed.

On the 28th of October, a detachment under command of Colonel Dyer left the main body, and the next day attacked the Indian village of Littefutchee, surprising it before daylight in the morning, destroying it, and bringing in twenty-nine prisoners as the first-fruits of the campaign.

This was the beginning of a series of battles which followed each other in as rapid succession as the starving condition of the army permitted. Jackson was now in the enemy's country, and within striking distance of his strategic points. How vigorously and persistently he struck, we shall see in the chapters which follow.

CHAPTER 16

The Battle of Tallushatchee

On the second day of November, Jackson learned that a considerable force of the enemy was gathered at Tallushatchee, an Indian town about ten miles from the Ten Islands. He had no sooner received this information than he ordered Coffee with about nine hundred men to attack the post.

Coffee marched on the moment, taking with him a company of friendly Indians, mostly Cherokees, under Richard Brown. To prevent errors the Indians in the expedition wore white feathers and deer-tails on their heads.

The expedition crossed the river a few miles above the Ten Islands, and advanced during the night, arriving in the immediate neighbourhood of the town about daybreak on the 3rd of November. The purpose was not merely to defeat but to destroy the Indian force, and therefore, instead of dashing at once into the town, Coffee divided his force in half, sending Colonel Allcorn with the cavalry to the right, while he himself, in company with Colonel Cannon, marched to the left around the place, keeping at a sufficient distance to avoid alarming the Indians.

When the heads of the two columns met, the town was entirely surrounded. Notwithstanding the caution with which this movement was executed, the Indians discovered the presence of the enemy when the troops were half a mile distant. They beat their drums and yelled in savage fashion, but remained on the defensive, awaiting the attack.

About sunrise, everything being in readiness, General Coffee sent two companies forward into the town, without breaking his circular alignment, instructing the officers in command of them to make an assault and bring on the action. The manoeuvre was altogether successful. As soon as the two companies made their attack, the Indians, confident that this was the whole of the assaulting column, rushed out of their houses and other hiding-places; and charged their assailants with great vigour. The companies of whites thereupon began falling back and the Creeks pursued them hotly. When the main line was reached, it delivered a volley into the midst of the advancing savages, and immediately charged them, driving them back in confusion to the shelter of their houses. Here the Creeks fought with the utmost desperation, refusing quarter, obstinately resisting when resistance was manifestly in vain, and choosing to die where they stood, rather than yield even to Coffee's overwhelming numbers.

General Coffee said in his report of the affair:

The enemy retreated, firing, until they got around and in their buildings, where they made all the resistance that an overpowered soldier could do. They fought as long as one existed; but their destruction was very soon completed. Our men rushed up to the doors of the houses, and in a few minutes killed the last warrior of them. The enemy fought with savage fury, and met death with all its horrors, without shrinking or complaining; not one asked to be spared, but fought as long as they could stand or sit. In consequence of their flying to their houses and mixing with their families, our men, in killing the males, without intention killed and wounded a few of the squaws and children, which was regretted by every officer and soldier of the detachment, but which could not be avoided.

Coffee counted one hundred and eighty-six dead bodies of Indians, and, as many of them fell in the grass and high weeds, where their bodies were not easily found, he expressed the opinion in his report that the number of killed did not fall short of two hundred, while his own loss was five men killed and forty-one wounded, most of the wounds being slight and none of them mortal. For the first time in the history of Indian warfare, the fighting force of the savages in this battle was utterly destroyed, not a single warrior escaping alive.

There were eighty-four prisoners taken, all of them being

women and children. Not only General Coffee, but his officers and men also, would gladly have ended the fight as soon as victory was theirs, sparing the warriors who had survived the first onset, and they constantly offered quarter not only to bodies of men who were fighting together, but to single individuals who were manifestly at their mercy, and to wounded warriors; but their offers of mercy were indignantly rejected in every case, and they therefore had no choice but to convert the battle into a massacre more complete than that which had occurred at Fort Mims, except that the women and children were spared; but this time the butchery was forced upon the victors against their will, while at Fort Mims the triumphant savages had willingly indulged in indiscriminate slaughter.

Coffee at once took up his return march and rejoined Jackson, who sent a brief despatch reporting the affair to Governor Blount, praising Coffee and his men in the strongest terms, and ending with that plaintive plea for food for his army, which was now constantly on his lips. He wrote:

> If we had a sufficient supply of provisions we should in a very short time accomplish the object of the expedition.

The most encouraging thing about this affair was the good conduct of the men. They manifested so little of the spirit of raw and undisciplined troops; they fought with so much coolness and steadiness, and went through the battle showing so few signs of that excitement which commonly impairs the efficiency of inexperienced soldiers, that their commander felt a confidence in them which justified him in attempting more than he would otherwise have dared in the circumstances.

Mr. Parton, in his Life of Andrew Jackson, preserves a story which grew out of this battle, and which so strongly illustrates the softer side of a stern soldier's character, that we may be pardoned for breaking the narrative to copy it here.

> On the bloody field of Tallushatchee was found a slain mother still embracing her living infant. The child was brought into camp with the other prisoners, and Jackson, anxious to save it, endeavoured to induce some of the Indian women to give it nourishment. 'No,' said they, 'all his relatives are dead; kill

him too.' This reply appealed to the heart of the general. He caused the child to be taken to his own hut, where among the few remaining stores was found a little brown sugar. This, mingled with water, served to keep the child alive until it could be sent to Huntsville, where it was nursed at Jackson's expense until the end of the campaign, and then taken to the Hermitage. Mrs. Jackson received it cordially, and the boy grew up in the family, treated by the general and his kind wife as a son and a favourite. Lincoyer was the name given him by the general. He grew to be a finely formed and robust youth, and received the education usually given to the planters' sons in the neighbourhood. Yet it appears he remained an Indian to the last, delighting to roam the fields and woods, and decorate his hair and clothes with gay feathers, and given to strong yearnings for his native wilds.

The boy did not live to reach manhood, however. In his seventeenth year he fell a victim to pulmonary consumption, and when he died his benefactor mourned him as bitterly as if he had been indeed his son.

CHAPTER 17

The Battle of Talladega

Where was General Cocke with the troops from East Tennessee all this time? It will be remembered that he was to muster twenty-five hundred men in his half of the state, while Jackson gathered a like number in the west, and marching southward the two were to form a junction in the Creek country. Meantime General Cocke had undertaken to procure in East Tennessee supplies for the whole force. The supplies, as we know, had not come, and Jackson had marched without them. Now he expected General Cocke daily, with his force and his supplies; but they came not, and Jackson was greatly disappointed.

The fact was that General Cocke had been delayed by precisely the same lack of breadstuffs that had embarrassed General Jackson. He had collected supplies, indeed, and ordered them forward by way of the river, but for lack of water they had not come, and at last, like Jackson, he began his march without them. He started south from Knoxville on the 13th of October, and after a considerable delay on the route, abandoned all hope of receiving the supplies, and depended thereafter upon such aid as the friendly Cherokees could give him in the way of furnishing provisions. General White had marched separately with his brigade, and when he joined General Cocke his men were in a starving condition.

While marching in a column separate from Jackson's, General Cocke was an independent commander. If he should join Jackson, whose commission was older than his own, the East Tennessee commander must become subordinate to the authority of Jackson. The fact that he did not form the contemplated union of forces, but acted separately, and the additional fact that his separate action led to a blunder which added greatly to the horrors of the war, caused Jackson great annoyance, and subjected General Cocke to the severest criticism. He was accused of an undue and culpable jealousy of Jackson, of self-seeking, and of perverse disobedience of orders. To all of this we shall come presently. The matter is mentioned now merely because it is necessary to know this much about it in order that we may properly understand the events to be immediately narrated.

As soon as Coffee's command returned from the Tallushatchee expedition, General Jackson resumed his march over a mountainous country toward the Ten Islands. Upon arriving at that point on the Coosa River, he began the construction of a fort as a centre of operations, and a defensive post at which his supplies—whenever he should happen to have any thing of that kind—could be protected by a comparatively small force. He adopted the usual method of fortifying against Indian assaults—inclosing a large space within a line of strong timber pickets, and building block-houses, storehouses, and other needed structures within. Here he was disposed to await the arrival of General Cocke, hoping that that officer would bring provisions of some sort with him, as the force at Fort Strother—that was the name given to the works at the Ten Islands—was now almost destitute of food and forage.

When Cocke was within three days' march of Fort Strother, his advance-guard, about one thousand strong, under command of General White, was within a very short distance, and General White sent forward a courier from Turkey Town reporting his arrival at that point, and asking for orders.

About this time there came into Jackson's camp a messenger, who brought news of a very important nature. He came from a little fort thirty miles away, at the Indian town of Talladega, on the spot where the modern town of Talladega stands. In that fort a handful of friendly Indians, about one hundred and fifty in number, had gathered to escape butchery at the hands of their hostile brethren. Here they were closely besieged by an Indian force one thousand strong, who, contrary to their usual practice, made no assault, but sought to starve out the little garrison. They surrounded the fort and maintained an unbroken siege line, confident that the plight and even the existence of the beleaguered fort were unknown to the whites, and confident, therefore, that no relief could be sent to them. They knew, too, that the supply of water, as well as of food, in the fort was very scant, and hence they had only to await the sure operation of starvation and thirst to do their work for them.

The messenger who came to Jackson to pray for the deliverance of the little band from their pitiable situation is described by some writers as an Indian, by others as a chief, and by still another he is said to have been a Scotchman who had lived for many years among the Indians as one of themselves. The last-named writer has evidently confused this case with another. Whoever and whatever he was, this man had escaped from the fort by a characteristic Indian stratagem. He had covered himself with a swine's skin, and wandered about like a hog in search of roots. In this way he managed to work his way at night through the lines of the besiegers, and when once beyond them he travelled as rapidly as possible toward Jackson's camp, and reported the state of affairs.

He arrived on the 7th of November, and Jackson at once began casting about for ways and means. He scarcely dared to march with his scanty supplies of food, and he scarcely dared to leave his post with an insufficient force to defend it; but he must rescue that band of friendly Indians at all hazards and at any cost. Their hard situation appealed to his pity; the cruelty of their foes appealed to the stronger stuff in his composition, arousing his anger and his disposition to wreak a righteous vengeance. There were reasons of polity, too, to move him to activity in their behalf. If they should be left to their fate, the discouragement of the friendly Indians everywhere would be great, and might be calamitous.

Jackson quickly considered all of these things and formed his resolution. General White was at Turkey Town at the head of about a thousand men. Jackson resolved to order him to march immediately upon Fort Strother, and to hold the place while the main army should be absent. There was great danger in leaving the post unguarded even for a brief time, but the occasion was so pressing that the resolute commander determined to take the risk, hoping that White would arrive in time to prevent disaster at the fort.

Having sent his order to White, he began his preparations for an immediate march with the whole effective force at the post.

Between midnight and one o'clock the next morning, November 8th, the column began its march, two thousand strong, eight hundred being mounted men. The task of fording the Coosa occupied the hours until the dawn of day, the horses of the cavalrymen being used for the transportation of the infantry across the stream.

A march of twenty-four miles consumed the day, and not long before dark General Jackson halted his men within six miles of the enemy, in order that they might rest. It was his purpose to resume the march after midnight, and attack the enemy early in the morning.

Thus far all had gone well, but here something like calamity overtook the commander in the shape of extremely bad news. A courier arrived bringing a despatch from General White, in which that officer informed Jackson that he could not obey the order given him to advance and protect Fort Strother, because of positive orders from his immediate superior, General Cocke, commanding him to return and rejoin the East Tennessee division of the army.

The state of facts which now confronted Jackson was most appalling. He was a long day's march from his fortified camp, with an impending battle on his hands; while his camp, to which alone he could retire when his present task should be done, was lying open and helpless, at the mercy of any band of Indians which might choose to attack it! Worse still, Jackson knew that the food supplies at the camp were exhausted, and as General White was not to come up with the provisions which he had promised to bring with him, Jackson saw that after fighting the Indians in his front he should be obliged to march his exhausted and hungry army back to a post where there was nothing for them to eat. His was a terrible dilemma, neither horn of which offered him hope. He expressed his anger with General Cocke and General White in forcible terms; but that did him no good, and the offending officers were not present to profit by the rebuke.

The Indians in his front probably had some provisions, enough at least for a meal, and Jackson determined to secure these at any rate, and at the same time to accomplish the purpose of his expedition.

Putting his army in motion very early in the morning he approached the Talladega town. When within half a mile of the foe he formed his line of battle, dividing the cavalry and placing half of it upon each wing. The advance was made slowly in the centre, so that the wings might gradually encircle the enemy, a movement much more difficult here than it had been at Tallushatchee, because of the greater numbers of the enemy, and because of their distribution over a wider area. For these reasons the plan of battle was less perfectly carried out on this occasion than on the former one, but it proved effective notwithstanding the difficulties which prevented its perfect execution.

At the proper moment a small body of troops was thrown forward from the centre to bring on the action. This force made a spirited attack, firing several successive volleys into the ranks of the surprised Indians, before a determined resistance was made to their attack. Then the Creeks charged upon them in force, and in accordance with the instructions they had received, the officers commanding the advance withdrew toward the main line, falling back in good order and at a moderate speed. We cannot do better than let General Jackson tell the rest of the story. In his report of the affair he said:

> The enemy pursued, and the front line was now ordered to advance and meet him; but, owing to some misunderstanding, a few companies of militia, who composed part of it, commenced a retreat. At this moment a corps of cavalry, commanded by Lieutenant-Colonel Dyer, which I had kept as a reserve, was ordered to dismount and fill up the vacancy occasioned by the retreat. This order was executed with a great deal of promptitude and effect. The militia seeing this, speedily rallied; and the fire became general along the front line, and on that part of the wings which was contiguous. The enemy, unable to stand it, began to retreat, but were met at every turn and repulsed in every direction. The right wing chased them, with a most destructive fire, to the mountains, a distance of about three miles, and, had I not been compelled, by the *faux pas* of the militia in the outset of the battle, to dismount my reserve, I believe not a man of them would have escaped. The victory, however, was very decisive: two hundred and ninety of the enemy were left dead, and there can be no doubt but many more were killed who were not

found. Wherever they ran they left behind traces of blood, and it is believed that very few will return to their villages in as sound a condition as they left them.

In the engagement we lost fifteen killed and eighty-five wounded; two of them have since died. All the officers acted with the utmost bravery, and so did all the privates, except that part of the militia who retreated at the commencement of the battle; and they hastened to atone for their error. Taking the whole together, they have realized the high expectations I had formed of them, and have fairly entitled themselves to the gratitude of their country.

Jackson's loss in wounded included General Pillow, Colonel Lauderdale, Major Boyd, and Lieutenant Barton; but of these only Lieutenant Barton died of his wounds. The friendly Indians rescued numbered one hundred and sixty men, with their women and children.

In writing that two hundred and ninety of the enemy were found dead, General Jackson dealt in round numbers. General Coffee, who seemed always to have an exacting curiosity in such matters, said in a letter which was written soon after the battle:

We have counted two hundred and ninety-nine Indians dead on the ground, and it is believed that many have not been found that were killed dead; but the battle-ground was so very large we had not time to hunt them up. It is believed that very few got clear without a wound.

General Coffee said also in this letter, which is preserved in the archives of the Tennessee Historical Society, that "the force of the enemy was a little upwards of one thousand warriors, picked men, sent forward to destroy our army." By dint of adding to the numbers of Indians known to have been killed in the two battles thus far fought as many more as he believed to have been killed, and assuming that the wounded equalled the killed in numbers, General Coffee arrived at the conclusion that the battles of Tallushatchee and Talladega had left the fighting force of the Creeks "a thousand men weaker" than when the campaign began. The calculation was scarcely a fair one, however; assumptions respecting dead men not found are necessarily unsafe, and as there were no wounded men at all left alive at Tallushatchee, the calculation respecting wounded men was of course founded upon an erroneous assumption, to say nothing of the fact that the only men wounded and not killed at Talladega were so slightly wounded that they succeeded in getting away, and hence could scarcely be accounted lost to the Creeks.

It is easy to pardon the enthusiastic general his slight overestimate of the damage inflicted upon the enemy, whom he was so earnestly anxious to defeat. The damage was great, certainly, and the success thus far attained had been secured at small cost in the matter of the lives of the white troops.

The object for which Jackson had marched from Fort Strother to Talladega was fully accomplished. The hostile Creeks in that quarter had been routed with heavy loss, and the little band of beleaguered friendly Indians were released from their dangerous and trying situation; but Jackson's army was hungry, and there was a prospect that actual starvation would presently overtake it. The little food that was found at Talladega was distributed among the men, sufficing to satisfy their immediate needs.

The pressing necessity of the hour now was to return with all possible haste to Fort Strother, which must not be left in its defenceless state a moment longer than was absolutely necessary; but an instantaneous beginning of the return march was wholly out of the question. The men had begun their toilsome journey at midnight between the 7th and 8th of November, had marched all day on the 8th, and, after a few hours' rest, had begun to march again a little after midnight, to go into battle early on the morning of the 9th. Now that the battle was done, they were utterly worn out, and must rest. Accordingly, the army went into camp for the night, after they had buried their dead comrades. The next day the return march was begun, and on the 11th of November the weary army arrived at their encampment.

The fort was unharmed, but it was destitute of provisions, and for a time it was with great difficulty that Jackson prevented a mutiny among the troops, whose only food was the meagre supply gleaned from the surrounding wilderness.

CHAPTER 18

General Cocke's Conduct

It is necessary now to explain the circumstances which left Fort
Strother without the garrison under General White, which General Jackson had provided for its defence during his absence, and
to show to what consequences this failure of the East Tennessee
commander to co-operate with General Jackson presently led. The
writers upon these historical events differ very widely in their judgment of the case, and most of them severely censure General Cocke,
attributing his conduct to an unworthy jealousy. His rank was the
same as that of General Jackson; but, as was said in a former chapter,
Jackson's commission was the older one, and hence if Cocke had
joined his "ranking officer," Jackson would have been in command
of the whole force. It was alleged at the time and afterward that
both the East Tennessee troops and their commander were jealous
of Jackson and his army, and envious of that army's success. To this
unworthy motive General Cocke's conduct has generally been attributed. Mr. Pickett, in his History of Alabama, gives an account of
the matter, which is substantially the same as those given by Drake
in his Book of the Indians, and by most other writers.

In that account he says, without doubt or qualification, that the
want of concert between the two divisions of the army grew:

.... out of a jealousy of the former (the East Tennessee division), and a strong desire to share some of the glory which
the latter had already acquired in the few battles they had
fought.

Mr. Parton, in his Life of Andrew Jackson, gives a different version of the affair, attributing General Cocke's course to his earnest-

ness in the cause, and his knowledge of certain facts which were unknown to General Jackson. To that we shall come presently; but while General Cocke's statement, upon which Mr. Parton founds his opinion, is certainly entitled to consideration, it must not be forgotten that General Cocke was under at least implied orders to join Jackson—orders which he was bound as a soldier to obey, whatever his judgment may have dictated; that whatever he may have known, there were two or three things which he did not know; that one of these things unknown to him—namely, the departure of Jackson from Fort Strother—made his obedience to orders very necessary to the successful execution of Jackson's plans; and that his want of knowledge of another fact led to the perpetration of a fearful outrage—the driving of Indians who were disposed to become peaceful into fierce hostility, and the increase of the ferocity of the war. It was General Cocke's business to obey his orders, expressed or necessarily implied. For reasons which he thought good, he neglected to do so, and great evil resulted.

On the march southward Cocke's army had destroyed two or three deserted Indian villages, but had had no encounter with the enemy. When General Cocke arrived within a few days' march of Fort Strother he detached General White and sent him to Turkey Town. Thence White marched to Tallushatchee, intending to attack the place, but he arrived there after Coffee had destroyed the force gathered at that point, although his visit was on the same day. As he was marching to join Jackson, it does not very clearly appear why General White did not follow Coffee to the camp of the main body. He returned to Turkey Town instead, and from that point reported to Jackson, as we have seen, just as the army was about to march upon Talladega. He was at once ordered to advance and replace Jackson's force at the fort, but before he could execute the order he received the instructions from General Cocke already referred to, directing him to turn back and join the East Tennessee division at the mouth of the Chattooga River. Believing that in a case of conflicting orders it was his duty to obey that which came from his immediate superior, General White obeyed Cocke rather than Jackson.

Cocke had determined upon a separate operation against the Hillabees, and sending White to one of the Hillabee towns, that officer surprised and destroyed it on the 18th of November, killing sixty of the Hillabees and taking two hundred and fifty prisoners, mostly women and children. Pickett says:

> The Hillabees, it is asserted, made not the slightest resistance. At all events, not a drop of Tennessee blood was spilt.

The unfortunate feature of this affair was that to the Indians it wore the appearance of the basest and cruellest treachery. These Hillabees had been great sufferers at Jackson's hands in the battle of Talladega, and becoming convinced by the result of that battle that resistance was useless, they determined to surrender and make peace. They sent Robert Grayson, an old Scotchman who had lived among them for many years, to Jackson's camp to sue for peace, proposing to lay down their arms, and to comply with whatever terms Jackson might impose upon them. As the object of the war was not to kill the Creeks in wantonness, but to secure peace and good conduct at their hands, Jackson properly regarded the proposed surrender of the Hillabee tribe as the richest fruit of the campaign. Accordingly, he sent Grayson back to them with a lecture, and an acceptance of their capitulation. He said to them:

> Upon those who are disposed to become friendly, I neither wish nor intend to make war; but they must afford evidences of the sincerity of their professions. The prisoners and property they have taken from us and the friendly Creeks must be restored. The instigators of the war and the murderers of our citizens must be surrendered.

While Jackson was yet rejoicing in the belief that his hard-fought battle at Talladega and the hardships endured upon that expedition had accomplished so much more than the mere defeat of the enemy there, his work was utterly undone by the ill-timed and unfortunate expedition of White against the Hillabees. These people knew nothing of the divided councils of the Tennessee army, and when White came down upon one of their towns, while their messenger was still absent upon his errand of peace, they naturally supposed that their assailants were Jackson's men, and that he had sent them as his relentless messengers to answer the Hillabee prayer for peace with the merciless stroke of the sword. Convinced that Jackson was implacable, and that no hope remained to them, the Hillabees fled from all their towns and joined the hostile forces, wherever bodies of them could be found. Drake says, in the Book of the Indians:

> The Indians thought they had been attacked by General Jackson's army, and that therefore they were now to expect nothing but extermination; and this was thought to be the reason why they fought with such desperation afterwards. And truly they had reason for their fears; they knew none but Jackson, and supposed now that nothing short of their total destruction would satisfy him, as their conduct exemplified on every occasion. They knew they had asked peace on any terms, and their immediate answer was the sword and bayonet.

In acting as he did, without first consulting with General Jackson and learning both the exact situation of affairs and the nature of his superior officer's purposes, General Cocke did wrong in a military sense. Of this there seems to be no room whatever for doubt or question, and as his wrong-doing led to disastrous results, it was altogether natural that both General Jackson and the historians should severely censure the offending officer, as they did; General Jackson being violently exasperated, as well he might be, when he learned the full results of the blunder.

In saying as we do, that General Cocke was clearly culpable for acting as he did, we do not necessarily imply that his course was dictated by the jealousy and envy to which it has been attributed, or indeed by unworthy motives of any kind. His motives may, perhaps, have been perfectly unselfish; his conduct the result merely of bad judgment, or of inaccurate notions of military duty; but to establish these facts is only to palliate, not to excuse his offence. It is unjust, however, in any discussion of these matters, to neglect the defence which General Cocke made of his conduct. That defence was made in the autumn of the year 1852, in a letter published in the *National Intelligencer*, and was prompted by the publication of certain criticisms upon General Cocke's conduct. In the letter he says:

> About the 1st of October I rendezvoused my troops at Knoxville, and they mustered into service; and on the twelfth day after, I took up the line of march. I encamped with my command on the banks of the Coosa, which was the divid-

ing line between the Cherokee and Creek Indians, where I was compelled to halt for want of provisions for my own command; and at no time after I left Knoxville had I more than five days' rations for my army. At this point I waited for supplies from the contractor, but owing to the low water they did not arrive, and I was compelled to procure supplies from the Cherokees as best I could. General White joined me with his brigade in a starving condition upon the second day after my arrival on the Coosa.

Mr. Parton offers the following comment upon this part of the letter and upon the situation:

It thus appears that while General Jackson was anxiously looking for supplies from General Cocke, General Cocke himself was as destitute as General Jackson. A junction of the two armies would have had the sole effect of doubling Jackson's embarrassments, inasmuch as he would have had five thousand men to feed in the wilderness instead of twenty-five hundred, and would have required twenty wagon-loads of provisions daily instead of ten. General Cocke knew this; knew that Jackson's anxiety for a junction had arisen from an expectation that the East Tennesseeans would bring supplies with them; did not know that Jackson's dash at Talladega had left Fort Strother unprotected—did not know any thing about the Hillabees' suing for peace, and Jackson's favourable reply to them.

This, we say, is at most only a palliation of the offence. General Cocke did not know, as Mr. Parton says, that Jackson's anxiety for a union of the two armies was due to his expectation that the East Tennesseeans would bring supplies with them, because that was not the fact. He did expect them to bring provisions, but his anxiety for a junction was not altogether on that account. He wanted White's men for a garrison for Fort Strother, and hence General Cocke only believed that which Mr. Parton assumes that he knew. Again, if the junction had been made, and the doubling of the number of men had embarrassed Jackson, it would have been easy for him to separate the forces again. Moreover, after the Hillabee expedition was ended, General Cocke was ready and willing to join Jackson, while the scarcity of provisions remained; if his reason for not forming the junction was good in the one case, it was good also in the other. Indeed, General Cocke has himself contradicted the plea which Mr. Parton makes in his behalf. While General White was still absent on the Hillabee expedition, General Cocke wrote a letter to Jackson, in which he said:

> I entertain the opinion that to make the present campaign as successful as it ought to be, it is essential that the whole force from Tennessee should act in concert. I have despatched all my mounted men, whose horses were fit for duty, on the Hillabee towns, to destroy them. I expect their return in a few days. I send the bearer to you for the sake of intelligence as to your intended operations, and for the sake of assuring you that I will most heartily agree to any plan that will be productive of the most good.

From the fact that he thus arranged to put himself within the range of Jackson's authority as soon as his Hillabee campaign should be ended, the inference is inevitable that General Cocke neglected to make the contemplated earlier junction in order that he might carry out this little scheme of his own. Inasmuch as a court-martial, composed of officers who, General Cocke says, were his bitterest enemies and Jackson's closest friends, fully acquitted the accused officer of guilt, it is only fair to the memory of a brave and conscientious soldier to believe that he acted for the good of the cause; that his anxiety to deal a blow at the Hillabees was prompted by a desire to serve the ends of the campaign, not by unworthy jealousy of Jackson; but beyond this it does not appear to be possible to go. We may properly acquit General Cocke of petty envy, and of conscious insubordination, but it is impossible not to see that his course was ill-judged as well as calamitous in its results, and it is impossible also to blame Jackson for his displeasure with his subordinate. The most that General Cocke establishes in his defence, which is elaborate, is that he acted in accordance with the unanimous opinion of his field officers; that he conscientiously believed that his course was the best one to be pursued in the circumstances, and that it was dictated solely by his earnest desire to serve the cause. The most that is proved against him appears to be, that he acted with smaller regard to strict military rules than an officer of his rank should have done. He was guilty of a blunder, not of a crime.

CHAPTER 19

The Canoe Fight

With the affairs already described, Jackson's campaign came to a halt by reason of his want of supplies, and on account of mutinous conduct upon the part of his men. For many weeks the Tennessee army did nothing, but remained at Fort Strother, while the war went on in other parts of the field. For the present, therefore, we leave Jackson, to follow the course of affairs elsewhere.

The autumn having brought with it the necessity of gathering what remained of the crops in that part of the country which lies on the Alabama and Tombigbee rivers, the settlers there did what they could to clear the country of prowling bands of Indians. They sent out bodies of armed men in different directions, and under protection of such forces as they could muster, began gathering the ripened corn. The danger of famine, if the corn should be allowed to perish in the fields, seems also to have aroused General Flournoy from his dream of strict adherence to law and treaty in his treatment of the Creeks. His predecessor, General Floyd, had refused, it will be remembered, to permit General Claiborne to invade the Creek Nation early in the war, when that officer confidently believed that he could speedily conquer a peace by pursuing that course. Flournoy now receded from the position then taken, so far at least as to order Claiborne to advance with his army and protect the citizens while they should gather their crops. He still ordered no resolute invasion of the Creek territory, for the purpose of transferring the seat of war to the soil of the enemy, and putting an end to the strife; but he ordered Claiborne to drive the Indians from the frontier, and even to follow them so far as the towns which lay near the border, instructing him to—

111

COL CALLER'S ROUTE TO BURNT CORN CREEK

. . . . kill, burn, and destroy all their negroes, horses, cattle, and other property, that cannot conveniently be brought to the depots.

General Flournoy, like General Floyd, appears to have been somewhat too highly civilized for the business in which he was engaged. Knowing, as he did, that Claiborne was fighting savages who had violated every usage and principle of civilized warfare, who were prowling about in the white settlements murdering every white man, woman, and child whom they could find, and who had committed the most horrible wholesale butchery at Fort Mims; knowing all this, and knowing too that an army from Tennessee was already invading the Creek country from the north, General Flournoy appears to have given Claiborne this half-hearted and closely-limited permission to fight the Creeks upon their own terms and their own soil with great reluctance and with apologetic misgivings. He set forth his conviction that even the little which he was now permitting Claiborne to do toward making the war real on the white side was not in accordance with the usages of civilized nations at war; but excused himself for his departure from those usages by citing the conduct of the enemy in justification of it. A stronger man than General Flournoy would have seen that the Creeks had turned complete savages, that they had begun a savage warfare for the extermination of the whites, and that such a war could be brought to an end only by the destruction of the white people whom he was set to protect, or by the prompt, resolute, and complete subjugation of the Creeks. Seeing this, such an officer would have seen that the Creeks could be conquered only by the invasion of their territory with fire and sword, and with no respect whatever for those rights which were theirs in peace, but which had been forfeited in the war. It seems incredible that General Flournoy, in such circumstances and with such an enemy to contend with, should have muddled his head and embarrassed his army with nice questions of the rights, duties, and usages of civilized warfare. This was so clearly not a civilized, but an especially savage war, that his hesitation, and the misgivings upon which that hesitation was founded, are wholly inexplicable.

Claiborne was quick to use the small liberty given him to

fight the Creeks, while the settlers, from their positions in the stockade forts, were already making frequent expeditions against vulnerable points.

Early in October, a body of twenty-five men, under Colonel William McGrew, went in pursuit of an Indian force, and attacked them resolutely on a little stream called Barshi Creek. The Indians were in considerable force, and despite the courage and determination of the whites the Creeks got the best of the affair, killing Colonel McGrew and three of his men, and putting the rest of the force to flight. Much better success attended another expedition, which was undertaken about this time, and which resulted in one of the most remarkable incidents of the war, a sort of naval battle on a very small scale, but one that was contested as heroically as the battle of the Nile itself. This was Captain Sam Dale's celebrated canoe fight, of which a writer has said:

> There has seldom occurred in border warfare a more romantic incident.... History has almost overlooked it, as too minute in its details for her stately philosophy. Yet for singularity of event, novelty of position, boldness of design, and effective personal fortitude and prowess, it is unsurpassed, if equalled, by any thing in backwoods chronicles, however replete these may be with the adventures of pioneers, the sufferings of settlers, and the achievements of that class who seem almost to have combined the life and manners of the freebooter with the better virtues of social man.

When Colonel McGrew's men returned after their unsuccessful conflict with the Creeks, the news they brought greatly incensed the people of Fort Madison, whose friends had fallen in that unlucky action. Believing that the main body of the Creeks was now south of the Alabama River, and fearing that they would destroy the buildings and the crops there, Captain Sam Dale, who had now nearly recovered from his severe wound received at the battle of Burnt Corn, organized an expedition for the purpose of clearing the lower country, if possible, of the hostile bands. The force which volunteered for this service consisted of seventy-two men. Thirty of them constituted Captain Richard Jones's company of Mississippi yauger men. The remainder were men of the neighbourhood, who volunteered for the expedition.

Among these volunteers were three whose participation in the canoe fight makes it necessary to introduce them particularly to the reader. One of them was a negro, whose name, Caesar, together with his good and gallant conduct on this occasion, are all that history has preserved with respect to him. Another was young Jeremiah Austill, the youth who carried despatches, as already related, between Colonel Carson and General Claiborne, when that service was most dangerous. The third was James Smith. We may best tell what is known of young Smith in the words of Mr. A. B. Meek, whose volume of sketches, from which we shall quote here, is unfortunately out of print. Mr. Meek writes thus:

> In Dale's command was a private soldier who already had a high reputation as an expert, daring and powerful Indian fighter. Born in Georgia in 1787, this scion of the universal Smith family was now a very stout, finely-proportioned man, five feet eight inches high, weighing one hundred and sixty pounds. Residing near Fort Madison, he took refuge there at the outbreak of the war. His fearless and adventurous character may be indicated by an incident. One day he determined to visit his farm, about eight miles distant, to see what injury the Indians had done. Proceeding cautiously, he came to a house in which he heard a noise, and, stealing up to the door, he found two Indians engaged in bundling up tools and other articles to carry them off. Levelling his gun at them he made them come out of the house and march before him toward the fort. In a thicket of woods the Indians suddenly separated, one on each hand, and ran. Smith fired at one of them and killed him, and, dropping his rifle, pursued the other, and, catching him, knocked him down with a light-wood[1] knot and beat out his brains.... This, and similar deeds of daring and prowess, gave to James Smith a high position among his frontier friends and neighbours.

Mr. Meek writes more fully of young Austill. He describes him as a youth nineteen years of age, dark, tall, sinewy, and full of youthful daring. The stories of his courageous performances were many,

1:"Light-wood" is a term used in the South to signify richly resinous pine, of the kind sometimes called "pitch-pine" in other parts of the country.

and during the war he won the special commendation of his superiors on many occasions for his bravery and his devotion to duty.

Dale marched from Fort Madison on the 11th of November, with Tandy Walker, a noted frontiersman, for his guide. Marching to the south-east, the column crossed the Alabama River at a point about thirty miles above Mims's ferry, and about twenty miles below the site of the present town of Claiborne.

Dale was thoroughly well acquainted with the habits of the Indians, among whom indeed he had lived frequently for long periods. He was therefore keenly alive to the necessity of unremitting vigilance, and, determined to suffer no surprise, he refused to permit any of his men to sleep during the night after his passage to the south-east bank of the river. During the next day he advanced up the river very cautiously, sending Austill, with six men, in two canoes which he had found, while the rest of the force marched through the woods on the bank.

At a place called Peggy Bailey's bluff the first signs of the presence of Indians were discovered. Following the trail well in advance of his men, Dale discovered ten Indians at breakfast. The first intimation these Indians had of the presence of white men on that side of the river came to them in the shape of a bullet from Dale's rifle, which killed one of the party, and caused the rest of them to abandon their provision pack, and flee precipitately through the woods.

Securing the abandoned provisions, Dale marched on a mile or two, but finding no further traces of Indians, he determined to recross the river and scour the country on the other side.

The work of crossing was necessarily slow. Only two canoes were to be had, and the river was nearly a fourth of a mile wide, but little by little the force was paddled across, until only about a dozen of the men remained with Dale on the eastern bank. These men were at breakfast when suddenly they were startled by a volley from the rifles of an Indian force. This force, as was afterward learned, was the advance party of about three hundred warriors. Dale and his handful of men protected themselves as well as they could among the trees, and returned the fire. Had the savages known the weakness of their force, they might easily have destroyed the little party by making a determined dash; but Dale and his men were so well concealed among the trees and in the bushes, that their enemies, in ignorance of their numbers, did not dare charge them. The nature of the ground served also to favour Dale. The river here had what is called a double bank—that is to say, there were two plateaus, one above the other, each breaking rather suddenly at its edge. These banks, covered with dense undergrowth, served the purpose of rude natural breastworks.

The first assault was made by about twenty-five or thirty of the savages, who were speedily joined by others, and Dale quickly saw that his position was an extremely critical one. The Indians must soon discover from the infrequency of the fire from the bank that the force there was small, and it was certain that they would make a charge as soon as this should be discovered—a charge which the dozen men there could not possibly withstand. Dale's first thought was of escape across the river to the main body of his little company; but this was clearly out of the question. There was but one canoe on his side of the river, so that to cross at all the little company on the bank must separate, half of it going over at one trip and half at another. If half of them should embark, the Indians, seeing the canoe in the river with its cargo of fugitives would know at once that the band on the bank was unable to resist them, and hence would destroy the men left behind before the canoe could return to bring them away.

Dale called to his men on the other side of the river to recross and render him assistance, but they seemed to be for the time fairly panic-stricken, so that none of them moved to answer the call. After a time their courage appeared to return, and eight of them manned a canoe and began the passage. When the man who led this detachment saw the great superiority of the Indian force, he became panic-stricken again and ordered a retreat, so that even this little attempt to reinforce Dale's tremendously overmatched company failed to bring relief.

Meantime a new danger appeared, coming this time upon the rear. A large canoe holding eleven Indian warriors shot out from the bank a little way up the river and paddled down to Dale's position. Here an attempt was made to land. Should this be accomplished, the fight must end at once in the destruction of the whole detachment on the river bank. To ward off this danger Dale was compelled to fight both ways—to the rear and to the front. He himself, with all of his men but three, kept up not a brisk, but a very destructive, fire in front, picking their men and shooting with all the precision of skilled marksmen; while Smith, Austill, and one other man devoted their attention to the warriors in the canoe, preventing them from approaching the shore.

Being kept thus at a distance, two of the most daring of the Indians in the canoe resolved to risk an attempt to swim ashore. Leaping overboard only their heads were exposed, of course; but Smith succeeded in sending a bullet into even that small target, killing one of the swimmers instantly. The other reached the bank, where he was met by Austill, who unluckily tripped and fell into the water, and before he could regain his footing the savage had escaped.

His escape brought matters to a head. Dale knew that this Indian had seen how small his force was, and that he would report its weakness, thereby making an immediate charge certain. He therefore resolved upon a desperate attempt. He called to his men, declaring his purpose to man the little canoe that remained with him, and attack the Indian canoe party. For this perilous service he asked who would volunteer. Smith, Austill, and the negro man Caesar at once offered themselves; and with this little force Dale speedily put his plan into execution. Caesar took the stern of the canoe as steersman, and the three white men grasped their paddles.

The Indians had fired all their ammunition away, else it would have gone hard with Dale when his own and his comrades' guns failed to fire as they did, because the powder in their pans had become wet. When this fact was discovered the two canoes were near each other, and Dale had no thought of flinching from the hand-to-hand conflict which must ensue between himself and his three companions on the one hand, and the nine remaining Indians on the other. He ordered Caesar to bring the canoe alongside the enemy's boat, and to hold it firmly there. As this was done the Indians leaped to their feet, with their war-clubs and knives, ready for the combat. When the boats touched, Dale instantly leaped into that of his enemy, for the double purpose of crowding the enemy close together and giving his own companions abundant room in which to swing their clubbed guns. It was a mere question of brute strength between men determined to club each other to death. Austill was knocked down with a war-club once, but recovered himself. Dale advanced in the boat, knocking over one Indian after another with his rapid blows. A few minutes sufficed to bring the action to a close.

It is said that the last of the Indians was a young warrior with whom Dale had lived and hunted as a friend before the outbreak of the war. This young Indian and his former friend now confronted each other in the boat. Dale recognized the man with whom he had sat at the camp-fire and passed long days in the hunt; he hesitated, and was about to lower his raised weapon when the young savage, calling him by the name he had borne among the Indians, which meant "Big Sam," cried, "Sam Thlucco, you are a man, I am another—now for it!" He spoke in the Muscogee tongue, with which Dale was familiar, and as he spoke he attempted to grapple with Dale, but the active white man was too quick of movement for him. Stepping back suddenly, he brained his Indian antagonist with a single blow, and the canoe-fight was ended. The nine Indians were corpses, and Dale had not lost a single man, although Austill was severely wounded in the head.

There was perilous work yet to do, however. The brave men in the boat had no thought of abandoning their friends on the bank. Their own guns were broken, and they were under a severe fire from the savages on shore, but in spite of this they cleared the large canoe by throwing the dead Indians overboard, and, with the two boats, paddled back to the bank under a galling fire, and brought off the remainder of the party in safety. If they had not conquered, they had at least baffled the Indians, inflicting considerable loss upon them without suffering any loss in their turn. That night the expedition returned to Fort Madison.

Dale was so typical a frontiersman, so perfect a model of the daring and wily warrior of the border, that as long as he lived he was a man about whom the interest of curiosity hung. A writer who knew him well wrote of him thus:

In person General Dale was tall, erect, raw-boned, and muscular. In many respects, physical and moral, he resembled his antagonists of the woods. He had the square forehead, the high cheek-bones, the compressed lips, and in fact the physiognomy of an Indian, relieved, however, by a firm, benevolent, Saxon eye. Like the red man, too, his foot fell lightly upon the ground and turned neither to the right nor left. He was habitually taciturn; his face grave; he spoke slowly and in low tones, and he seldom laughed. I observed of him what I have often noted as peculiar to border men of high attributes—he entertained the strongest attachment for the Indians, extolled their courage, their love of country, and many of their domestic qualities; and I have often seen the wretched remnant of the Choctaws camped around his plantation and subsisting on his crops. In peace they felt for him the strongest veneration; he had been the friend both of Tecumseh and Weatherford; and in war the name of 'Big Sam' fell on the ear of the Seminole like that of Marius on the hordes of the Cimbri.[2]

2: From a sketch by General John H. F. Claiborne, published in the Natchez (Miss.) *Free-Trader*, on the occasion of Dale's death in the year 1841.

CHAPTER 20

The Battle of Autosse

When the call was made by General Claiborne upon Tennessee for assistance, a similarly earnest appeal was sent to Georgia, and the response from that State was equally prompt. The troops raised there were under command of General Floyd, who had been superseded in the command of the Department of the South-west by General Flournoy some months earlier. General Floyd was an energetic soldier, and he quickly found work to do.

It will be remembered that as soon as Red Eagle learned that he would not be permitted to attack and burn Mobile he turned his attention to the country north and east of the Creek Nation, and sent two bodies of his warriors to harass the borders, one force threatening Tennessee and the other seeking to find some vulnerable point on the Georgia frontier. Jackson's advance with an overwhelming force and his vigorous blows at Tallushatchee and Talladega compelled the Creeks to abandon their designs upon Tennessee and stand upon the defensive. They saw the full significance of his advance, and knew that he had come not merely to garrison forts and protect settlers, but to carry the war to the heart of the Creek Nation, and to throttle the Creek power in its stronghold. This was what Claiborne wanted to do by a resolute movement from the south, and there can be little doubt that if he could have had permission to do so he would have saved the Tensaw and Tombigbee settlements from the worst of their sufferings, by making the Creeks the hunted rather than the hunters, precisely as Jackson saved the people of Tennessee by an aggressive policy. The other column, which threatened Georgia, was met in like manner by General Floyd, and with like results.

Floyd's army consisted of nine hundred and fifty militiamen and four hundred friendly Indians, part of them being Cowetas under command of Major McIntosh, one of the half-breeds whom High Head Jim had planned to kill as a preparation for the war, and the rest Tookabatchas under Mad Dragon's Son. Floyd was better equipped than Jackson had been in his first battles, having some small pieces of artillery with him.

Having learned that a large force of the Creeks was at High Head Jim's town, Autosse, on the south-east side of the Tallapoosa River, about twenty miles above the point at which that stream unites with the Coosa, General Floyd marched against them in the latter part of November. McAfee, who is usually a very careful historian, gives the 28th of September as the date, but this is clearly wrong. Crossing the Ockmulgee, Flint, and Coosa rivers under the guidance of a Jewish trader named Abram Mordecai, Floyd arrived in the neighbourhood of Autosse early in the morning on the 29th of November.

His plan of battle was precisely the same as that which Coffee had adopted at Tallushatchee, and Jackson at Talladega—that is to say, he planned to surround the town and destroy the fighting force within; but in this case the scheme miscarried. In the first place, McIntosh and Mad Dragon's Son were ordered to cross the river and cut off retreat to the opposite shore, and they failed to do what was required of them. Whether this was due to the unforeseen difficulties of crossing, as the Indians alleged; or to the reluctance of the Indians to swim the river on a cold, frosty morning, as some historians say; or to a failure of their courage, as was charged at the time—there are now no means of determining, and it is not important. It is enough to know that they did not cross the river as ordered, and hence when the attack was made the bank of the stream opposite the town was unguarded.

This was not the only way, however, in which the original plan of attack was prevented. The real position and strength of the Indian force had been misapprehended, and when, early in the action, this was discovered, General Floyd was obliged to alter his disposition of troops accordingly. The advance was made as soon as there was sufficient light, on the morning of the 29th of November, with Booth's battalion on the right, Watson's on the left. The flanks were guarded by riflemen, and Thomas with his artillery accompanied Booth's battalion. Booth was instructed to march until he could rest the head of his column upon the little creek at the mouth of which the town stood, while Watson was to stretch his column around to the left in a curve, resting its left flank upon the river just below the town. If this could have been done as intended, and the friendly Indians had occupied the opposite side of the river, the encircling of the place would have been complete; but besides the failure of the Indians another difficulty stood in the way. Instead of one town there were two, the second lying about a quarter of a mile further down the river, immediately in rear of the position to which Watson had been ordered.

To avoid the danger of an attack in the rear of his left flank, which might have resulted disastrously, General Floyd sent Lieutenant Hendon with Merriweather's riflemen, three companies of infantry and two of dragoons to attack the lower town, while he threw the remainder of the army, now reinforced by the friendly Indians under Mad Dragon's Son and McIntosh, against the larger upper town.

The fighting began about sunrise, and speedily became extremely severe. The prophets had enchanted the place, making it sacred ground, and they had assured the warriors that any white force which should attack them would be utterly exterminated. In this belief the savages resisted the attack with terrible determination, contesting every inch of the ground which they believed to be sacred.

Soon after the battle began, the artillery—an arm which was particularly dreaded by the Creeks with something of superstitious horror—was brought forward and unlimbered. Its rapid discharges soon turned the tide of battle, which until now had not gone against the Indians. When the Indians began to waver before the cannon-shot, Major Freeman with his squadron of cavalry charged and broke their lines. They were closely pressed by the infantry, while the friendly Indians who had now crossed the creek cut off retreat up the river, leaving the broken and flying Creeks no road of escape except across the river. At nine o'clock both towns were in flames, and there was no army in Floyd's front. He was victor in the action, and his success in attacking a sacred stronghold was certain to work great demoralization among the superstitious Creeks; but prudence dictated a retreat nevertheless. The country round about was populous with Indians, and the force which fought at Autosse although broken was not destroyed. It was certain that if the army should remain in the neighbourhood it would be constantly harassed, and perhaps beaten by the superior force which the Creeks could speedily muster.

Besides all this, Floyd had only a scanty supply of provisions, and his base of supplies was sixty miles away, on the Chattahoochie River. He determined, therefore, to begin his return march as soon as he could bury his dead and arrange for the care of his wounded, of whom he was himself one.

The return march was perhaps hastened by the determination and spirit of the Indians, who, notwithstanding their defeat, attacked Floyd's rear within a mile of their burned town on the day of the battle. The attack was made with spirit, but the numbers of the Indians were not sufficient to enable them to maintain it long.

In this battle of Autosse Floyd lost eleven white men killed and fifty-four wounded, besides some losses among his friendly Indians. Coffee not being there to count the dead Creeks, the exact number of the slain warriors of the enemy was not ascertained, but it was estimated at about two hundred.

CHAPTER 21

The Battle of the Holy Ground

General Claiborne construed as liberally as he dared the order from General Flournoy which permitted him to drive the Creeks across the border, and to pursue them as far as the neighbouring towns. He adopted the frontier notion of nearness when deciding whether or not a particular town that he wanted to strike was sufficiently near the dividing line between the white settlements and the Creek Nation.

His orders were to establish a fort at Weatherford's Bluff, and to remain in that neighbourhood until he should be joined by Jackson's army and the Georgia troops, who were now advancing under command of General Floyd.

The force with which he advanced to execute this order was a motley one. There were three hundred volunteers, who were the main reliance of the commander. There was a small dragoon force, composed of good men. Pushmatahaw, the Choctaw warrior, with his followers accompanied the expedition, and a small force of militiamen completed the little army.

Arriving at Weatherford's Bluff on the 17th of November, Claiborne proceeded without delay to build a stockade fort inclosing nearly an acre of ground, within which he built three block-houses, while for defence against an assault from the river side of the encampment he established a battery on the bank. The work, when finished, was christened Fort Claiborne, and from it the present town of Claiborne on the same spot inherited the commander's name.

Here, on the 28th of November, Claiborne was reinforced by the Third Regiment of United States Infantry, under command of Colonel Russell, and in order that concert of action might be secured, he wrote hence to General Jackson at the Ten Islands, reporting the situation of affairs on the southern side of the field, and informing the Tennessee commander, of whose starvation he had heard, that abundant supplies of food awaited his coming.

His activity knew no bounds. He sent trustworthy messengers to Pensacola to learn the situation of affairs there, and ascertained through them that the British were there with a considerable fleet and abundant supplies both for the Indians and for their own troops, whose presence there threatened a descent upon Mobile or New Orleans. He wrote at once to Governor Blount, of Tennessee, informing him of these facts. He sent messengers also to Mount Vernon, instructing Colonel Nixon, who commanded there, to garrison Fort Pierce, a little post a few miles from the ruins of Fort Mims, and suppress a recently awakened activity among the Indians in that quarter.

The alertness of Claiborne's intelligence and his unwearied devotion to duty made him an especially fit man for the important charge that was laid upon him. A close study of his career shows him to have been indeed so capable a man in military affairs, that we may fairly regret that his field of operations was too small and too remote from the centres of American life to permit him to secure the fame which he fairly earned.

General Claiborne was not thinking of fame, however, but of making fierce war upon the Creeks and reducing them to subjection. He knew that Red Eagle with a strong force was at Econachaca, or the Holy Ground, and he determined to attack him there. The Holy Ground was one hundred and ten miles from Fort Claiborne, and it could not be, with any strictness of construction, considered a "neighbouring" town; but the order which restricted Claiborne's excursions into the Creek Nation to the neighbouring towns was couched in terms which did not admit of precise definition, and as he really wanted to march to the Holy Ground, the gallant general determined to regard it as a place within his immediate neighbourhood. He did not know, in truth, precisely where it was, and there were neither roads nor paths through the woods to guide him to it, but he believed, with Suwarrow, the Russian commander, that a general can always find his enemy when he really wants to do so, and in this case Claiborne very earnestly wished to find and to fight Weatherford.

Accordingly he prepared to march. He was in poor condition for such an undertaking certainly, his force being weak in numbers, ill assorted, and in fact rather unwilling to go. Nine of his captains, eight lieutenants, and five ensigns sent him a written remonstrance against what they believed to be the mad undertaking. These officers directed their commander's attention to several ugly facts with respect to his situation. They reminded him that the weather was cold and inclement; that the troops were badly shod and insufficiently supplied with clothing; that there was scarcely a possibility of feeding them regularly upon so long a march into the literally pathless forest; and finally that the term of service for which many of the men had enlisted would soon come to an end.

The remonstrance was earnest, but perfectly respectful. The officers who signed it assured General Claiborne that if he should adhere to his determination they would go with him without murmuring, and do their duty. As there was nothing set forth in the remonstrance which Claiborne did not know or had not duly considered already, it made no change in his mind. He set his motley army in motion, determined to take all responsibility, dare all dangers, and endure all hardships for the sake of accomplishing the purpose which he had so long cherished, of carrying the war into the centre of the Creek Nation. How heavy the load of responsibility which he thus took upon himself was, and how firm his courage in assuming it must have been, we may understand when we reflect that defeat in his attempt would certainly have subjected him to a charge of criminal and reckless disobedience of orders in undertaking such an expedition at all. No such charge was ever preferred, because officers are not usually haled before a court-martial for winning battles.

The force with which he set out consisted of the Third Regiment of United States troops, under Colonel Russell; a squadron of cavalry, commanded by Major Cassels; one battalion of militia, led by Major Smoot, whom the reader will remember as one of the leaders at the battle of Burnt Corn; Colonel Carson's Mississippi volunteers, and Pushmatahaw's Choctaws, to the number of one hundred and fifty, making a total of about one thousand men. Dale was a captain now in Smoot's command, and accompanied the expedition in that capacity.

The march was begun early in December, through a country without roads, infested with Indians whose force could never be guessed, and in weather which was extremely unfavourable. Toilsomely the column advanced north-eastwardly, or nearly so, to a point eighty miles from Fort Claiborne, in what is now Butler County, Alabama. There Claiborne took the precaution to build a stockade fort, which he named Fort Deposit, and placed within it his baggage, his artillery, his supply wagons, and his sick men.

Leaving this fort with a garrison of one hundred men, Claiborne marched on toward the Holy Ground, which lay some thirty miles away. His men speedily consumed the three days' rations of flour which they had drawn before beginning the march from Fort Deposit, and when the army arrived at the Indian stronghold its supply of pork, the only remaining article of food, was nearly exhausted. Whatever was to be done must be done quickly, in order that the troops might not starve before reaching Fort Deposit on the return march.

The Holy Ground was a newly-established town, upon a spot chosen by Red Eagle because of its natural strength as a defensive position. It lay upon the eastern bank of the Alabama River, just below what is now Powell's Ferry, in the present Lowndes County, Alabama. The site of the town was a high bluff overlooking the river, and protected on the land side by marshes and deep ravines.

Here Red Eagle had gathered his forces in considerable strength, and hither had fled the remnants of various defeated bodies of Creeks, with their women and children. The prophets Sinquista and Josiah Francis, who were present, declared the soil to be sacred, and assured their comrades that no white troops would be permitted by the Great Spirit to cross the swamps and ravines which surrounded it.

Red Eagle, having more faith in defensive works than in supernatural interferences at the behest of his prophets, whose characters he probably understood pretty accurately, added to the natural strength of the place by picket and log fortifications, making it as difficult to assault successfully as he could.

In this central camp of refuge there were as many as two hundred houses, and during the two or three months which had elapsed since the town was established many of the prisoners taken by the Indians in battle had been brought hither and murdered. When Claiborne advanced to attack the place, preparations were making in the public square for the burning of a number of unfortunate captives, among whom were one white woman, Mrs. Sophia Durant, and several half-breeds.

Claiborne arrived on the 23rd of December, and made his dispositions for the assault without delay. He advanced in three columns, leading the centre in person. The Indians, as soon as they learned of Claiborne's approach, made preparations for defence. They carried their women and children across the river and concealed them in the thick woods on the other side.

The savages made the first attack, falling violently upon the right column of Claiborne's force under Colonel Carson. The onset was repulsed after a brief engagement, the Indians becoming panic-stricken for some reason never explained, and retreating. Weatherford led the attack, and for a time contested the field very stubbornly; but his men failing in courage in spite of all that he could do, he was powerless to maintain his ground.

Major Cassels, who with his squadron of cavalry had been ordered to occupy the river bank, failed to do so, and fell back instead upon Carson's regiment; and that gallant officer, seeing the gap thus produced, advanced his line and occupied the ground. Meantime, however, the mischief had been done. Cassels's failure had left a road of escape open to the Indians at the critical moment, and hundreds of them fled and swam the river to the thick woods on the other side.

When the Indian line broke and the retreat began, the nature of the ground, crossed as it was by ravines and dotted with marshes, made any thing like vigorous and systematic pursuit impossible. Perhaps their consciousness that escape by flight was easy helped to induce the Indians to abandon the struggle when they did. However that may be, they fled, and Weatherford could not rally them. Seeing himself left alone, with no followers to maintain the struggle, he was forced to choose between flight and capture. Flight, however, was not now by any means easy. He was mounted upon a superb gray horse which carried him in his flight with the speed of the wind, but he was not long in discovering that Carson had closed the gap through which he had hoped to escape. His enemies were on every side of him but one, and on that side was the high bluff. The story of what he did, as it is commonly told, is a very marvellous one. A bluff about one hundred feet high at the Holy Ground is shown to travellers, who are told that Red Eagle, seeing no other way of escape, boldly dashed spurs into his horse and forced him to make the fearful leap to the river below! As the story is usually told in print it is somewhat less marvellous, but is still sufficiently so to serve the purposes of a popular legend. It is that a ravine passed through the upper part of the bluff, reducing its height to about fifty feet, and that Red Eagle made a leap on his horse from that height. This version of the story is so gravely told in books that are not romances, that the author of the present volume once cited it in print in justification of an incident in a work of fiction, believing at the time that the legend was well authenticated. In examining authorities more carefully, as he was bound to do before writing of the incident in a serious work of this kind, he finds that the leap was much less wonderful than has been represented. Mr. Pickett, in his History of Alabama, gives us the following account, which he assures us he had from Red Eagle's own lips:

Coursing with great rapidity along the banks of the Alabama, below the town, on a gray steed of unsurpassed strength and fleetness, which he had purchased a short time before the commencement of hostilities of Benjamin Baldwin, late of Macon County, came at length to the termination of a kind of ravine, where there was a perpendicular bluff ten or fifteen feet above the surface of the river. Over this with a mighty bound the horse pitched with the gallant chief, and both went out of sight beneath the waves. Presently they rose again, the rider having hold of the mane with one hand and his rifle firmly grasped in the other. Regaining his saddle, the noble animal swam with him to the Autauga side.

The battle over, Claiborne found his loss to be one man killed and six others wounded. Thirty Indians were found dead on the ground. The number of their wounded is not known. Claiborne destroyed the town, with everything in it.

The army was now reduced almost to starvation, their only food being a little corn, which they parched and ate as they could. An alarm having been given by a party of men who were sent up the river in pursuit of fugitives, however, Claiborne marched in that direction during the night of December 24th, and pitched his tent on Weatherford's plantation, where he ate his Christmas breakfast of parched corn. Having destroyed all the buildings in the neighbourhood, Claiborne's work in this region was done, and he hastened back to Fort Deposit, where he fed his troops before beginning his return march to Fort Claiborne. The army had been nine days without meat.

The term of service for which Carson's volunteers had enlisted had now expired, and as soon as the column arrived at Fort Claiborne the men were mustered out. In a letter to the Secretary of War, Claiborne reported that these men went home nearly naked, without shoes, and with their pay eight months in arrears. Their devotion to the cause, as it was shown in their cheerfulness and good conduct during their toilsome march, was, in view of all the circumstances, highly honourable to them. Leaving Colonel Russell in command of Fort Claiborne, General Claiborne returned to Mount Vernon, partly because he had fully accomplished all that his orders from Flournoy permitted him to do, and partly because the discharge of his Mississippi volunteers had reduced his army to sixty men, and even these had but a month longer to serve!

Colonel Russell was no sooner left in command at Fort Claiborne than he instituted proceedings designed to fix the responsibility for the sufferings of the men during the campaign and for the blunder at the Holy Ground where it belonged. He ordered a court of inquiry in each case, but Major Cassels was permitted to escape censure on the ground that his guide had misled him. For the failure of the food supply the contractor was held responsible, as it was shown that General Claiborne had given him strict orders to provide abundant supplies for the expedition.

In order that the story of the Fort Claiborne army may be finished here before returning to the Ten Islands and following Jackson through his more important part of the campaign, we may depart for the moment from the chronological order of events to tell the story of an unsuccessful attempt which Colonel Russell made to invade the Creek Nation from Fort Claiborne, in the February following the events already described.

It was Colonel Russell's purpose to march to the Old Towns on the Cahawba River, and thence to attack the Indians wherever he could find them, establishing his base of supplies at that point. He provided a barge, loaded it with food for the troops, and putting Captain Denkins in command of it, with a piece of artillery as his armament, he directed that officer to ascend the Alabama River to the mouth of the Cahawba River, and thence to make his way up the Cahawba to Old Towns, where the army would meet him. Then, with his regiment reinforced by an infantry company from the neighbourhood of Fort Madison under command of Captain Evan Austill, and a cavalry company commanded by Captain Foster—the two forming a battalion under the lead of Sam Dale, who was now a Major—Colonel Russell marched to the appointed place of rendezvous. There he learned that the barge had not arrived, and as he had marched with but six days' provisions his situation was a critical one. To hasten the coming of the barge he despatched a canoe manned by Lieutenant Wilcox and five men in search of Captain Denkins. This party, while making its way down the river, travelling at night and hiding in the cane on the banks by day, was attacked by Indians. Lieutenant Wilcox and three of his companions were made prisoners, the other two escaping and making their way through many hardships to the settlements, where they arrived in a famished condition.

Captain Denkins had passed the mouth of the Cahawba River by mistake, and had gone a considerable distance up the Alabama River before discovering his error. When he did discover it, he knew that it was now too late for him to think of carrying out his original instructions. He knew that before he could possibly reach the Old Towns, the army would be starved out and compelled to retreat.

He therefore determined to return to Fort Claiborne. On his way down the river he discovered the canoe, and found in it Wilcox scalped and dying, and his two companions already dead.

Meantime Colonel Russell had waited two days at the Old Towns for the coming of the barge, and then, being wholly without provisions, began his return march, saving his army from starvation by killing and eating his horses on the route.

CHAPTER 22

How Jackson Lost His Army

We now return to General Jackson's camp at Fort Strother, near the Ten Islands. The situation there was bad from the time of the Talladega expedition, and it grew steadily worse. The army was nearly starved, and Jackson was sharing their hunger with them. When a few lean kine were secured, seeing that the supply was sufficient only to give to each man a very scant portion, Jackson declined to take any part of the beef for his own table, and took some of the entrails instead, saying with cheerfulness that he had always heard that tripe was nutritious and savoury food. He lost no opportunity to secure such provisions as could be had from the surrounding country, but these were barely sufficient to keep famine at bay from day to day, and Jackson busied himself with the writing of letters to everybody who could in any way contribute to hasten forward adequate supplies. He wrote to one contractor, saying:

I have been compelled to return here for the want of supplies when I could have completed the destruction of the enemy in ten days; and on my arrival I find those I had left behind in the same starving condition with those who accompanied me. For God's sake send me with all despatch plentiful supplies of bread and meat. We have been starving for several days, and it will not do to continue so much longer. Hire wagons and purchase supplies at any price rather than defeat the expedition. General White, instead of forming a junction with me, as he assured me he would, has taken the retrograde motion, after having amused himself with consuming provisions for three weeks in the Cherokee Nation, and left me to rely on my own strength.

Nothing that the perplexed commander could do or say or write, however, could help him. Day by day food became scarcer, poorer, and more difficult to get, and the men were becoming mutinous, as volunteers are sure to do when left to starve in inaction. If the enemy had appeared in his immediate neighbourhood, Jackson would certainly have cured all the disorders of the camp and removed its discontent by giving the men constant occupation for their minds in conflicts with the foe. As it was, there was neither food nor fighting to be had at Fort Strother, and General Jackson did not dare to attempt a march upon the nearest Indian stronghold, about sixty miles away, without supplies.

Not many days had passed after the return to the Ten Islands when information reached Jackson that the men of the militia regiment intended to return to their homes with or without permission, and that they had appointed the next day as the time of starting. Luckily he believed that he could still depend upon the volunteers. He knew, too, that in this matter he had to deal with bodies of men, not with individuals. The power of public sentiment, which in this case was corps sentiment, was the power arrayed against him. He knew that the men would not desert singly, that their pride would restrain them from desertion unless they could act together, each being sustained by the opinion and the common action of all his fellows. The militia had determined to march home in a body; Jackson determined to restrain them in a body.

On the appointed day he called the volunteers to arms, and at their head placed himself in the way of the mutinous militiamen. He plainly informed the men that they could march homeward only by cutting their way through his lines, and this was an undertaking which they were not prepared for. Being unable to overcome Jackson, they had no choice but to yield to him and return to their tents, which they did at once, with what cheerfulness they could command.

The volunteers whose power Jackson was thus able to use in arresting the departure of the militia were scarcely less discontented than they. On the very day on which they stopped the march of the militia they resolved themselves to go home, and prepared to depart on the following morning. Jackson had information of what was going on, and he prepared to reverse the order of things by using the militia in their turn to oppose the volunteers. The militia having returned to their duty obeyed the commands of their general, and opposed a firm front to the mutinous volunteers. The affair wore so much of the appearance of a practical joke that it put the whole force into momentary good-humour.

With his men in this mood, however, Jackson knew that he had merely gained a very brief time by his firmness, and that the discontent of which the mutiny was born existed still in undiminished force. He therefore sent the cavalry to Huntsville to recruit their horses, first exacting a promise that they would return as soon as that end could be accomplished—a promise which the men afterward violated shamelessly. He then called all the officers of the army together, and, after giving them all the facts in his possession upon which he founded the confident hope that provisions in plenty would soon arrive, he made a speech to them, trying to win them back to something of their old devotion to duty. He had good reason to believe that supplies both of meat and of breadstuffs were now actually on their way to him, and his chief present purpose was to gain time, to persuade his followers to patience and obedience for the two or three days which he thought would end the period of short rations. According to Eaton's report of the speech, Jackson said to his officers:

What is the present situation of our camp? A number of our fellow-soldiers are wounded and unable to help themselves. Shall it be said that we are so lost to humanity as to leave them in this condition? Can anyone, under these circumstances and under these prospects, consent to an abandonment of the camp; of all that we have acquired in the midst of so many difficulties, privations, and dangers; of what it will cost us so much to regain; of what we never can regain—our brave wounded companions, who will be murdered by our unthinking, unfeeling inhumanity? Surely there can be none such! No, we will take with us when we go our wounded and sick. They must not, shall not perish by our cold-blooded indifference. But why should you despond? I do not; and yet your wants are not greater than mine. To be sure we do not live sumptuously; but no one has died of hunger or is likely to die. And then how animating are our prospects! Large supplies are at Deposit, and already are officers despatched to hasten them on. Wagons are on the way; a large number of beeves are in the neighbourhood, and detachments are out to bring them in. All these resources cannot fail. I have no wish to starve you, none to deceive you. Stay contentedly, and if supplies do not arrive in two days we will all march back together, and throw the blame of our failure where it should properly lie; until then we certainly have the means of subsisting, and if we are compelled to bear privations, let us remember that they are borne for our country, and are not greater than many, perhaps most, armies have been compelled to endure. I have called you together to tell you my feelings and wishes. This evening think on them seriously, and let me know yours in the morning.

To this appeal the response was not satisfactory. The militia indeed agreed to remain during the stipulated two days, and promised that if the expected provisions should come within that time they would cease to murmur, and go on with the campaign; but the volunteers were now wholly given over to mutiny. They insolently informed General Jackson that they were going to march back to the borders of Tennessee, and that if he refused to yield immediately to their will in the matter, without waiting for the allotted two days to expire, they would go without permission and would use force if necessary to accomplish that end.

There can be no doubt whatever about the nature of the reply which Jackson would have made to this message if he had had even a small force upon which he could rely at his back. In that case the volunteers must have chosen between submission to his will and a battle with him. As it was, he was one man against the whole force. He could not oppose the mutinous volunteers with arms, and he felt that he must in some way prevent the abandonment of all that had been gained in the campaign. He therefore resorted to a compromise, which he hoped would solve the perplexing problem. He commanded the militia and one regiment of the volunteers to remain in the fort as a garrison, and ordered the other volunteer regiment to march toward Fort Deposit until it should meet the provision train, and then to countermarch and return with it. In this way he lost immediately only one half of the volunteers, winning the rest of them to his proposition for a delay of two days; and even the regiment which had been sent away might yet return with the provisions, as the lack of food was the only plea that had been urged in defence of the mutiny.

The discontent really lay much deeper than that: it had come as much from idleness in camp and from home-sickness as from hunger, and it had eaten into the soldierly characters of the men, honeycombing them with sedition and insubordination; but while the plea of starvation remained to them the men urged no other, and Jackson's memory of their courage and good conduct on former occasions, led him to hope that with this cause of trouble removed the trouble itself would disappear.

When the two days of waiting had passed, and no supplies had come, a new difficulty lay in Jackson's path, namely, his own voluntary promise. He had asked for two days' delay, promising to permit the men to march away if food did not arrive within that time. The promise now fell due and the men exacted its fulfilment. In his sore distress he could do nothing further to compel obedience. He had even relinquished his right to command the men to remain and his privilege to bargain for further delay. He must let them go now, but there was no reason why any of them who chose to do so might not voluntarily remain to defend the fort. It was a slender hope, but Jackson was grasping at straws now. He set out to seek volunteers, declaring that if even two men should consent to stay with him he would not abandon Fort Strother and the campaign, but would stay there and wait for the coming of reinforcements. One of his captains at once offered himself as one of this army of two, and by an earnest effort they succeeded in swelling the number of volunteers to one hundred and nine men. This was all that was left of Jackson's army, and the campaign lay mostly before him. A man of less stubborn resolution would have despaired; but Jackson held on in the hope of gaining strength after awhile and gathering men enough around him to make a resumption of operations possible.

He permitted the rest of his troops to leave the post, first exacting a promise that they would return if they should meet the supply train, and in order the more effectually to enforce this demand Jackson accompanied the column, leaving his army, one hundred and nine strong, to hold the fort until his return.

JACKSON CONFRONTING THE MUTINEERS

Twelve miles from the fort the column met the provision train. Jackson called a halt and ordered rations to be distributed to the men. It was now his turn to insist upon the faithful fulfilment of a promise. He had kept his word in permitting his men to abandon Fort Strother at the time appointed; he could now, with especially good grace, insist that the men should keep their promise and return with the provision train.

Now for the first time the mutiny began to assume its true colours. With stomachs filled with good beef and bread—for a large drove of beef cattle was with the provision train, and Jackson had given the men beef rations—it was no longer possible to urge hunger in excuse for abandonment of duty; but the men had set out intending to go home, and they had no thought of relinquishing that intention merely because the excuse by which they had justified their conduct would no longer serve their purpose.

When ordered to take up the line of march toward the fort the men rebelled and started homeward instead.

Then ensued one of the most impressive scenes in Jackson's career. Raving with rage, his thin lips set and his frame quivering with anger, the commander's face and mien were terrible. His left arm was still carried in a sling, and the hardships, hunger, fatigue, and ceaseless anxiety to which he had been subject ever since he quitted his sick-bed to come upon this campaign had not made his wasted frame less emaciated; he was a sick man who ought to have been in bed: but the illness was of the body, not of the soul. The spirit of the man was now intensely stirred, and when Jackson was in this mood there were few men who had the courage to brave him.

Riding after the head of the column, he placed himself with a few followers in front of it, and drove the men back like sheep. Then leaving the officers who were with him he rode alone down the road, until he encountered a brigade which was drawn up in column, resolved to conquer its way by a regular advance against any body of men who might oppose its homeward march. If a company or a battalion had undertaken to arrest the march of these men there would have been a battle there in the road without question. They were prepared to fight their comrades to the death; they were ready to meet a force equal to their own. They met Andrew Jackson instead—Andrew Jackson in a rage, Andrew Jackson with all the blood in his frail body boiling; and that was a force greatly superior to their own.

Snatching a musket from one of the men Jackson commanded the mutineers to halt. He broke forth in a torrent of vituperation, and declared that they could march toward home only over his dead body; he declared, too, with an emphasis which carried conviction with it, that while he could not, single-handed, overcome a brigade of armed men, he at least could and would shoot down the first man who should dare to make the least motion toward advancing.

The men were overawed, terrified, demoralized by the force of this one resolute man's fierce determination. They stood like petrified men, not knowing what to do. It was now evident that no man there would dare to make himself Jackson's target by being the first to advance. Jackson had beaten a brigade, literally single-handed, for he had but one hand that he could use.

By this time General Coffee and some staff officers had joined Jackson, and now a few of the better disposed men, seeing their general opposing a brigade of mutineers, ranged themselves by his side, prepared to assist him in any encounter that might come, however badly overmatched they might be. The mutineers were already conquered, however, and sullenly yielding they were sent back to the fort.

CHAPTER 23

The Plan of the Mutineers

Having thus succeeded in sending what remained of his army back to Fort Strother, with abundant food at least for present uses, Jackson hastened to Fort Deposit and succeeded there in effecting arrangements for a constant supply of bread and meat.

Then he mounted his horse and rode back to Fort Strother, determined to collect what force he could without delay, and by vigorous measures to bring the campaign to a speedy and successful end.

His first measure was to order General Cocke to join him with the East Tennessee troops, saying in his letter to that officer that if he could arrive at Fort Strother by the 12th of December, bringing with him all the provisions he could gather, the Creeks could be crushed within three weeks. This was a most inspiriting prospect, and Jackson was apparently all the more elated because of his recent depression.

His good fortune was destined to be short-lived, however. He had scarcely reached Fort Strother on his return from Fort Deposit when he discovered that his volunteers were planning a new mutiny, or, as they stoutly maintained, were preparing to leave him with legal right and justice on their side.

The state of the case may be briefly summed up as follows: These volunteers had been mustered into service on the 10th of December, 1812, the terms of their enlistment being that they should serve for one year within the next two years, unless sooner discharged; that is to say, they were to be discharged as soon as they should have served a year; or, if their actual service in the field should not amount to a full year they should be discharged on the 10th of December, 1814. They were called into service when Jackson made his march with them to Natchez, which has been spoken of in a former chapter. After a few months, their services not being needed, they were dismissed from actual service to their homes, subject, however, to a call at any time until their time of service should expire.

Under this enlistment they were recalled to the field in September, 1813, as we have seen, and were under obligation to serve for a sufficient time to complete their term of one year in the field; but as it had been supposed when they were enlisted that their services would be needed continuously for a year, they had thought little about the alternative condition. They now held that their enlistment would expire just one year after it had begun—that is to say, on the 10th of December, 1813, a date now at hand. They were determined to permit no allowance to be made for the months which they had passed at home, and insisted that as they had enlisted for one year they would go home when the year should end.

In this demand for discharge the officers, who should have been the men's instructors in such a case, made the matter hopeless by joining the discontented soldiery. With their colonels and majors and captains to second them, the men were doubly certain to persist in their interpretation of the contract of service.

Not long before the disputed date the colonel of one of the volunteer regiments laid their case before Jackson in a letter, in which he assured him that the volunteers would demand their honourable discharge from service on the 10th of December, the anniversary of their enlistment. The appeal made in this letter was an adroit effort to play upon next to the strongest feeling in Jackson's heart—his fatherly affection for the men who had followed him into battle. We say next to the strongest feeling in his heart, because the strongest was, undoubtedly, his desire to serve his country by accomplishing the utter suppression of the Creeks. The colonel told Jackson that the volunteers looked to their loved and honoured general to protect them in this their right, and to secure justice to them; that they lamented the necessity of leaving the field at such a time, but that their families and their private affairs required their return to their homes; that upon him, to whom they looked with reverence as to a father, depended the question whether, after their hard service under his leadership, they should be permitted to go home with the certificates of honourable discharge to which they were entitled, or should be forced to carry with them the ill-repute of deserters. He was strongly implored not to reward their devotion to the cause and to him by fixing this brand of disgrace upon them and their children after them.

The appeal was adroit we say, and a masterly piece of special pleading; but the officer who wrote it must have known when he did so that the demand which he sought to enforce was unjust; that even if it had been just, Jackson had no more authority than he himself had to grant it; and that the disputed question had already been submitted formally and fully to the Secretary of War, who had decided it adversely to the men, and had accompanied that decision by the assurance that as the matter was governed by an express act of Congress, no power short of that of the national legislature—neither the Secretary nor the President himself—was competent to change the terms of the enlistment, or to discharge the troops until either they had given a year to actual service, or the two years during which they were subject to a call had expired. For the men, and perhaps also for the subordinate officers, there may have been the excuse of an honest misunderstanding, but for this colonel, whose letter shows him to have been a man of high intelligence, there can have been no excuse at all.

Jackson replied to this letter in one of the ablest documents which has come from his hand. Eaton has preserved it in his Life of Jackson, and Mr. Parton has copied it. Let us see what the commander, touched without doubt by the *argumentum ad hominem* that was used, had to say by way of answer:

I know not what scenes will be exhibited on the 10th instant, nor what consequences are to flow from them, here or elsewhere; but as I shall have the consciousness that they are not imputable to any misconduct of mine, I trust I shall have the firmness not to shrink from a discharge of my duty.

It will be well, however, for those who intend to become actors in those scenes, and who are about to hazard so much on the correctness of their opinions, to examine beforehand with great caution and deliberation the grounds on which their pretensions rest. Are they founded on any false assurances of mine, or upon any deception that has been practised toward them? Was not the act of Congress, under which they are engaged, directed by my general order to be read and expounded to them before they enrolled themselves? That order will testify, and so will the recollection of every general officer of my division. It is not pretended that those who now claim to be discharged were not legally and fairly enrolled under the act of Congress of the 6th of February, 1812. Have they performed the service required of them by that act, and which they then solemnly undertook to perform? That required one year's service out of two, to be computed from the day of rendezvous, unless they should be sooner discharged. Has one year's service been performed? This cannot be seriously pretended. Have they then been discharged? It is said they have, and by me. To account for so extraordinary a belief, it may be necessary to take a review of past circumstances.

More than twelve months have elapsed since we were called upon to avenge the injured right of our country. We obeyed the call. In the midst of hardships, which none but those to whom liberty is dear could have borne without a murmur, we descended the Mississippi. It was believed our services were wanted in the prosecution of the just war in which our country was engaged, and we were prepared to render them. But though we were disappointed in our expectations we established for Tennessee a name which will long do her honour. At length we received a letter from the Secretary of War directing our dismission. You will recollect the circumstances of wretchedness in which this order was calculated to place us. By it we were deprived of every article of public property; no provision was made for the payment of our troops or their subsistence on their return march; while many of our sick, unable to help themselves, must have perished. Against the opinion of many I marched them back to their homes before I dismissed them. Your regiment, at its own request, was dismissed at Columbia. This was accompanied with a certificate to each man, expressing the acts under which he had been enrolled and the length of the tour he had performed. This it is which is now attempted to be construed 'a final discharge.' But surely it cannot be forgotten by any officer or soldier how sacredly they pledged themselves, before they were dismissed or received that certificate, cheerfully to obey the voice of their country, if it should re-summon them into service; neither can it be forgotten, I dare hope, for what purpose that certificate was given; it was to secure, if possible, to those brave men, who had shown such readiness to serve their country, certain extra emoluments, specified in the seventh section of the act under which they had engaged, in the event they were not recalled into service for the residue of their term.

Is it true, then, that my solicitude for the interest of the volunteers is to be made by them a pretext for disgracing a name which they have rendered illustrious? Is a certificate, designed solely for their benefit, to become the rallying word for mutiny? Strange perversion of feeling and of reasoning! Have I really any power to discharge men whose term of service has not expired? If I were weak or wicked enough to attempt the exercise of such a power, does any one believe the soldier would be thereby exonerated from the obligation he has voluntarily taken upon himself to his government? I should become a traitor to the important concern which has been entrusted to my management, while the soldier who had been deceived by a false hope of liberation would be still liable to redeem his pledge. I should disgrace myself without benefiting you.

I can only deplore the situation of those officers who have undertaken to persuade their men that their term of service will expire on the 10th. In giving their opinions to this effect they have acted indiscreetly and without sufficient authority. It would be the most pleasing act of my life to restore them with honour to their families. Nothing could pain me more than that any other sentiments should be felt toward them than those of gratitude and esteem. On all occasions it has been my highest happiness to promote their interest, and even to gratify their wishes, where with propriety it could be done. When in the lower country, believing that in the order for their dismissal they had been improperly treated, I even solicited the government to discharge them finally from the obligations into which they had entered. You know the answer of the Secretary of War: that neither he nor the President, as he believed, had the power to discharge them. How then can it be required of me to do so?

The moment it is signified to me by any competent authority, even by the Governor of Tennessee, to whom I have written on the subject, or by General Pinckney, who is now appointed to the command, that the volunteers may be exonerated from further service, that moment I will pronounce it with the greatest satisfaction. I have only the power of pronouncing a discharge, not of giving it, in any case—a distinction which I would wish should be borne in mind. Already have I sent to raise volunteers on my own responsibility, to complete a campaign which has been so happily begun, and thus far so fortunately prosecuted. The moment they arrive, and I am assured that, fired by our exploits, they will hasten in crowds on the first intimation that we need their services, they will be substituted in the place of those who are discontented here. The latter will then be permitted to return to their homes with all the honour which, under such circumstances they can carry along with them. But I still cherish the hope that their dissatisfaction and complaints have been greatly exaggerated. I cannot, must not, believe that the 'volunteers of Tennessee,' a name ever dear to fame, will disgrace themselves and a country which they have honoured, by abandoning her standard as mutineers and deserters; but should I be disappointed and compelled to resign this pleasing hope, one thing I will not resign—my duty. Mutiny and sedition, so long as I possess the power of quelling them, shall be put down; and even when left destitute of this, I will still be found in the last extremity endeavouring to discharge the duty I owe my country and myself.

CHAPTER 24

Jackson's Second Battle
With His Own Men

When troops unused as these men were to systematic obedience make up their minds to abandon the service they are of very
little account thereafter, as soldiers. If one pretext for mutiny and
desertion fails them, they quickly find another, as the men had
done in this case. While famine lasted, famine was the best possible excuse for wishing to go home, and the men thought of no
other. They even protested their devotion to the cause and their
willingness to remain in service if food could be found for them;
but no sooner were their mouths stopped with abundant supplies
of beef and bread than they tried to leave, as has been described,
without any pretext whatever. Failing in that, they picked this
flaw, or this pretended flaw, in their contract of enlistment, and
Jackson probably knew that so far as their restoration to the condition of good soldiers was concerned, he was wasting words in
arguing the case; but it was necessary to detain these men until
the others for whom he had sent to Tennessee should arrive to
take their places. They were useless for anything like offensive
operations, else he would have marched with them at once toward the Creek strongholds; but while they should remain at Fort
Strother he could depend upon them to defend that post against
any assault that might be made upon it, simply because in the
event of an attack they must defend themselves, and to do that
would have been to defend the fort.

Jackson had ordered the enlistment of a new force to take the
place of these discontented men, but until the new army should
come he was bent upon keeping the old one.

Precisely what arrangements he had made to meet trouble on the 10th of December we have no means of knowing. He was not permitted to wait for the coming of that day. On the evening of the 9th, word was brought to him that the men were already strapping their knapsacks on their backs and getting ready to march immediately.

It was time to act. Jackson issued one of the shortest of all his proclamations, ordering all good soldiers to assist in putting down the mutiny. Then he ordered the militia to parade at once under arms. Placing his cannon in a commanding position, he drew up the militia in line of battle and confronted the mutinous volunteers.

Riding to the front he made a speech to the volunteers, beginning by assuring them that they could march only over his dead body; that he had done with entreaty, and meant now to use force; that they must now make their choice between returning to their tents and remaining quietly upon duty, and fighting him and his troops right where he stood; the point, he said, could be decided very quickly by arms if they chose to submit the question to that kind of argument. He told them, too, that he was expecting new troops to take their places, and that until these new troops should arrive not a man present should quit the post except by force.

He was now terribly in earnest, and bent upon no half-way measures. He had drawn his men up in line of battle, not as a threat, but for purposes of battle. He was ready to fight, and meant to fight, not defensively, but offensively. He wanted no negotiation, asked no man upon what terms he would submit. He had dictated the terms himself and meant now to enforce them. He had given the volunteers a choice—either to remain peaceably until he should send them home, or to fight a battle with him right there in the road and right then on the 9th of December; he had offered them this choice, and they must choose and say what their choice was. When he ended his speech the volunteers stood grimly, sullenly silent. They did not offer to advance, but that was not enough. They must say whether they would remain and obey, or accept battle. If they would promise to remain without further attempts of this kind, he was content; if not, the battle would begin.

"I demand an explicit answer," he said; and no reply coming, he turned to his artillerymen and ordered them to stand to their guns with lighted matches.

It was now a question merely of seconds. Jackson gave the men time to answer, but not many moments would pass before he would speak the only words which were left to him to speak—the words "commence firing," those words which in every battle are the signal for the transformation of iron or brazen guns from harmless cylinders of metal into bellowing monsters, belching fiery death from their throats.

There was silence for a moment—that awful silence which always precedes the turmoil of battle, doing more to appal men than all the demoniac noises of the contest do; then a murmur was heard as of men hastily consulting; then the officers of the volunteer brigade stepped a pace to the front and delivered the answer which Jackson had demanded.

They had made their choice, and the answer was that they would return to duty, and remain at the fort until the new men should come, or until their commander should receive authority to discharge them.

This affair of the 9th of December, 1813, is nowhere set down in the list of Jackson's battles; but nowhere did he win a more decided victory or display his qualities as a great commander to better advantage.

CHAPTER 25

Jackson Dismisses His Volunteers

Jackson had not deceived himself with respect to these mutinous men. He knew very well that their usefulness as soldiers was
hopelessly gone, and he had no thought of undertaking a campaign
with them. Even before this last trouble came he had abandoned all
hope of this, and had ceased to regard the army he had with him
as worth keeping, except as a garrison for Fort Strother, during
the period of waiting for a new army to be raised to take its place.
It was his purpose to send this army back to Tennessee as soon as
he could replace the men with others fit to fight with, and to get
those others he was working in every possible way. He had sent to
Tennessee for the enlistment of a new force, and had written to
everybody he knew there who had aught of influence—preachers,
doctors, lawyers, and men of affairs—urging them to stir the enthusiasm of the young men and persuade them to volunteer. He
had already ordered General Cocke to join him with his force, and
that officer had promised to do so immediately. As this would give
him a sufficient garrison for the fort almost immediately, Jackson
determined to send home at once every man who could not be
stirred to a proper sense of his duty, every man who could not
be induced, by a fair and earnest statement of the case, to remain
voluntarily and finish the campaign. In order to separate any such
sheep, if there were any, from the homesick goats, the commander
on the 13th of December issued a final appeal, which was read to
the troops. It was as follows:

> On the 12th day of December, 1812, you assembled at the
> call of your country. Your professions of patriotism and abil-
> ity to endure fatigue were at once tested by the inclemency

of the weather. Breaking your way through sheets of ice you descended the Mississippi and reached the point at which you were ordered to be halted and dismissed. All this you bore without murmuring. Finding that your services were not needed, the means for marching you back were procured; every difficulty was surmounted, and as soon as the point from which you embarked was regained, the order for your dismissal was carried into effect. The promptness with which you assembled, the regularity of your conduct, your attention to your own duties, the determination manifested on every occasion to carry into effect the wishes and will of your government, placed you on elevated ground. You not only distinguished yourselves, but gave to your state a distinguished rank with her sisters, and led your government to believe that the honour of the nation would never be tarnished when entrusted to the holy keeping of the volunteers of Tennessee.

In the progress of a war which the implacable and eternal enemy of our independence induced to be waged, we found that without cause on our part a portion of the Creek Nation was added to the number of our foes. To put it down, the first glance of the administration fell on you, and you were again summoned to the field of honour. In full possession of your former feelings, that summons was cheerfully obeyed. Before your enemy thought you in motion you were at Tallushatchee and Talladega. The thunder of your arms was a signal to them that the slaughter of your countrymen was about to be avenged. You fought, you conquered! Barely enough of the foe escaped to recount to their savage associates your deeds of valour. You returned to this place loaded with laurels and the applause of your country.

Can it be that these brave men are about to become the tarnishers of their own reputation, the destroyers of a name which does them so much honour? Yes, it is a truth too well disclosed that cheerfulness has been exchanged for complaints. Murmurings and discontents alone prevail. Men who a little while since were offering up prayers for permission to chastise the merciless savage, who burned with impatience to teach them how much they had hitherto been indebted to our forbearance, are now, when they could so easily attain their wishes, seeking to be discharged. The heart of your general has been pierced. The first object of his military affections and the first glory of his life were the volunteers of Tennessee. The very name recalls to him a thousand endearing recollections. But these brave men, these volunteers, have become mutineers. The feelings he would have indulged, your general has been compelled to suppress; he has been compelled, by a regard to that subordination so necessary to the support of every army, and which he is bound to have observed, to check the disorder which would have destroyed you. He has interposed his authority for your safety—to prevent you from disgracing yourselves and your country. Tranquillity has been restored in our camp; contentment shall also be restored. This can be done only by permitting those to retire whose dissatisfaction proceeds from causes that cannot be controlled.

This permission will now be given. Your country will dispense with your services if you no longer have a regard for that fame which you have so nobly earned for yourselves and her. Yes, soldiers! You who were once so brave, and to whom honour was so dear, shall be permitted to return to your homes, if you still desire it. But in what language, when you arrive, will you address your families and friends? Will you tell them that you abandoned your general and your late associates in arms within fifty miles of a savage enemy, who equally delights in shedding the blood of the innocent female and her sleeping babe as that of the warrior contending in battle? Lamentable, disgraceful tale! If your dispositions are really changed, if you fear an enemy you so lately conquered, this day will prove it. I now put it to yourselves; determine upon the part you will act, influenced only by the suggestions of your own hearts and your own understandings. All who prefer an inglorious retirement shall be ordered to Nashville, to be discharged as the President or the Governor may direct. Those who choose to remain and unite with their general in the further prosecution of the campaign can do so, and will thereby furnish

a proof that they have been greatly traduced, and that although disaffection and cowardice have reached the hearts
of some, it has not reached theirs. To such my assurance is
given that former irregularities will not be attributed to
them. They shall be immediately organized into a separate
corps, under officers of their own choice; and in a little
while it is confidently believed an opportunity will be afforded of adding to the laurels you have already won.

If these men had had a single spark of soldierly spirit left in
them—if the manhood itself had not all gone out of them—such
an appeal as this would have shamed them into their duty. It is
incredible that men who had once had spirit enough to volunteer in the service of their country should have lost it so utterly
that they could resist this plea to their pride, their duty, and their
regard for their own good name; but such was the fact. Out of
the whole brigade, officers and men, only one was found with
manliness enough to stay. That one man was a Captain Wilkinson,
the mention of whose name is only a just tribute to his soldierly
manhood. The rest were no longer men in spirit, but homesick
wretches, lusting for the flesh-pots of Tennessee, the ease, the in-
dolence, the comfort of home.

Public opinion is particularly strong in a new country, where
every man's history is known to all his neighbours, and few men
in such a case can successfully brave it. Public opinion in Tennessee sharply condemned these volunteers for their abandonment
of the service upon a mere technicality, at a time when the enemy
was in their front. How sorely they smarted under the taunts of
their neighbours we may easily imagine; and when they could silently endure the censure no longer, they prepared a plea in their
own justification, which was published in March of the following
year. This plea was offered in the form of a statement, signed by
the brigadier-general who commanded the disaffected brigade,
one colonel, two lieutenant-colonels, two majors, an *aide-de-camp*,
and the brigade-quartermaster. These officers in their statement
recount the history of their service, and rest their case upon the
dates used in their muster-rolls, and the technicality that in dismissing them after their Natchez expedition Jackson had used the
word "discharge" instead of "dismiss." They assert that they and

their men were fully and finally discharged at the end of that expedition, and explain their readiness to answer the call to march against the Creeks, when Jackson assembled them a second time, by a confession that they thought they saw a chance to secure pay for service not rendered. They declare that they returned to the service, believing that their term could only last till the 10th of December in any case, and that by doing so they could compel the government to give them soldiers' pay for all the time which they had passed at home.

Read carelessly, their plea seems to palliate their misconduct; read at all carefully, it adds to their shame.

CHAPTER 26

How Jackson Lost the Rest of His Army

Having begun the work of getting rid of men upon whom he could not depend for active service, Jackson was disposed to complete it as speedily as possible, in order that he might resume the active operations of the campaign, knowing precisely what he could count upon in the way of an army and governing his measures accordingly.

He had counted upon General Cocke's force for at least half his strength, but here again he was doomed to disappointment. General Cocke came, it is true, according to the appointment, and brought an army of two thousand men with him; but they were three-months' men, and they had already served more than two months! General Cocke has declared in a printed letter that he had asked these men to give up the thought of going home at the expiration of their term of service, and voluntarily remain until the end of the campaign, and that the men had promised him to do so. He expressed in that letter surprise, not unmixed with indignation, that Jackson did not take them at their word; but when we remember what Jackson had just gone through, and reflect that these men would have ceased to be soldiers and become citizens when their time should expire; that their promise to remain till the end of the campaign would have had no binding force whatever; that they would have had the fullest right, individually or in bodies, to abandon the army at any moment, however critical the situation might be; and that Jackson would have had absolutely no authority over them, even to command obedience to orders in camp or battle, we cannot wonder that he declined to begin a campaign in the wilderness against a savage and wily foe, with an army which might dissolve at any moment and go home, and which, even while it should remain with him, would be free to disobey orders at its own sweet will. Campaigns are not successfully carried on, battles are not won, with mobs. Jackson meant to have an army before setting out again to crush the Creeks, and accordingly he sent Cocke's men home, retaining only Colonel Lillard's regiment as a temporary garrison for the fort.

He then ordered General Cocke to return to East Tennessee and enlist a new force, and urged the returning men to volunteer again as soon as they should have provided themselves at home with suitable clothing for a winter campaign.

It was his hope that two thousand men or more would be secured in East Tennessee and a like number in West Tennessee, and with such a force he could march into the Creek Nation and crush the savages, he believed, within a very brief time.

General Cocke obeyed the order very reluctantly, as he has himself told the public. His confidence in his men was so great, that he thought it unnecessary and unwise to dismiss them and search for others to take their place. He did as he was bidden, however, returning to East Tennessee and speedily securing a new force two thousand strong. These men volunteered for six months, and were mustered into service in time to march on the 17th of January.

On the march, however, these six-months' men learned that the new levies from the western part of the State—men between whom and the East Tennesseeans a wretched jealousy prevailed—were to be enlisted for only three months, and this bred sore discontent in General Cocke's camp. General Cocke met this difficulty resolutely, and in a published letter he has given an account of what he did.

> I overtook the troops at the Lookout Mountain, when I found a dissatisfaction among the troops amounting almost to mutiny. They declared their determination to return home at the end of three months. I made them a speech, in which I told them that if they left the army without any honourable discharge, they would disgrace themselves and families; that much of their time had already expired, and for all the good they could do, if they intended to leave at the end of three

months they had better go home then, but appealed to their magnanimity and patriotism to go on like brave men and good soldiers, and serve until the expiration of the term for which they were ordered into service.

These troops were certainly not in a mood to become soldiers fit for the work they had to do. Meantime the work of enlistment in West Tennessee had gone on very slowly and unsatisfactorily, and even Coffee's troopers, whom Jackson had sent to Huntsville to recruit their horses, exacting a promise from them that they would return as soon as they should accomplish that object, had broken faith and deserted in a body in spite of all that their gallant leader could do to restrain them.

Even this was not the end of Jackson's troubles. The men whom he had retained from Cocke's command were ready to leave as soon as their term of service should expire, and the date of its expiration was near at hand. This would diminish the force in Fort Strother from fourteen hundred to six hundred men. These six hundred were militiamen, and now, as if to break down what remained of Jackson's hopes, these troops managed to find an excuse for quitting the service and going home presently. The act of the legislature by which they had been called into service was bunglingly drawn, and upon examining it the militia officers discovered that nothing whatever had been said in the law with respect to the length of time for which they should serve. Then the question arose, How long have these men engaged to serve? The men held that as no term was set by the law the lawgivers must be held to have meant the shortest time for which it was customary to call out the militia, namely, three months, and that time would end on the 4th of January. Jackson, on the other hand, held that the law set no other limit to the term of service, because it meant that the service should continue as long as the war did. The men had been called out, he said, to suppress the Creeks, and their term of service would end when they had done that, and not before—whether that should be three months or three years after their enlistment. Jackson had fourteen hundred men, of whom eight hundred had an unquestioned right to quit in the middle of January, while the remaining six hundred asserted their right to retire at the beginning of that month. The new East Tennessee troops who were on their way to

157

him had enlisted for six months, but, as we know, were determined to serve only half of that term, a considerable part of which had already expired. Never was a commander in a sorer strait. Sent to fight a campaign and held responsible for its success, he was denied an army with which to fight at all. His commanding general urged him to activity, on the ground that the British must at any cost be shorn of the strength they had sought to secure by stimulating Indian hostilities; the British were already in Florida, threatening Mobile and New Orleans; the Seminoles in the Spanish province and the runaway negroes there were ready to take up arms and assail the Georgia borders; while in the North and West the war was prosecuted by the enemy with untiring perseverance.

But what was Jackson to do? The troops he had were about to leave him, and it began to appear that no others were likely to come to him. Even Governor Blount advised him to yield to the demands both of the six-months' volunteers who wanted to quit the service at the end of three months, and of the militia who wanted to quit almost immediately. Governor Blount sent Jackson a letter in which he urged this course upon him, advising him to regard the campaign as at an end, retire to the borders of Tennessee and protect that state as well as he could, abandon the attempt to raise a new force by enlisting volunteers, and quietly wait until the National Government should provide him with an army by ordering a draft or by some other means. Governor Blount believed that he had no authority to raise further forces, and that any attempt which he might make to do so must injure rather than help the service.

Then Jackson rose to the occasion, and showed that he was no less able as a debater than as a fighter. He wrote a letter to Governor Blount which changed the whole face of affairs, converted that executive officer to views the opposite of those that he had held, and led to the creation of a new army, or rather of two new armies, one being a temporary supply of short-term men, with whom Jackson did some work, and the other coming immediately to take its place. This letter, for the text of which we are indebted to Mr. Parton, is called by that writer "the best letter he ever wrote in his life—one of those historical epistles which do the work of a campaign." Jackson wrote:

Had your wish that I should discharge a part of my force and retire with the residue into the settlements assumed the form of a positive order, it might have furnished me some apology for pursuing such a course, but by no means a full justification. As you would have no power to give such an order, I could not be inculpable in obeying, with my eyes open to the fatal consequences that would attend it. But a bare recommendation—founded, as I am satisfied it must be, on the artful suggestions of those fireside patriots who seek in a failure of the expedition an excuse for their own supineness, and upon the misrepresentations of the discontented from the army, who wish it to be believed that the difficulties which overcame their patriotism are wholly insurmountable—would afford me but a feeble shield against the reproaches of my country or my conscience. Believe me, my respected friend, the remarks I make proceed from the purest personal regard. If you would preserve your reputation or that of the State over which you preside, you must take a straightforward, determined course, regardless of the applause or censure of the populace, and of the forebodings of that dastardly and designing crew who at a time like this may be expected to clamour continually in your ears. The very wretches who now beset you with evil counsel will be the first, should the measures which they recommend eventuate in disaster, to call down imprecations on your head and load you with reproaches.

Your country is in danger; apply its resources to its defence. Can any course be more plain? Do you, my friend, at such a moment as the present, sit with your arms folded and your heart at ease, waiting a solution of your doubts and definitions of your powers? Do you wait for special instructions from the Secretary of War, which it is impossible for you to receive in time for the danger that threatens? How did the venerable Shelby act under similar circumstances, or rather under circumstances by no means so critical? Did he wait for orders to do what every man of sense knew, what every patriot felt to be right? He did not; and yet how highly and justly did the government extol his manly and energetic conduct! and how dear has his name become to every friend of his country!

You say that an order to bring the necessary quota of men into the field has been given, and that of course your power ceases; and although you are made sensible that the order has been wholly neglected, you can take no measure to remedy the omission. I consider it your imperious duty, when the men called for by your authority, founded upon that of the government, are known not to be in the field, to see that they be brought there; and to take immediate measures with the officer who, charged with the execution of your order, omits or neglects to do it. As the executive of the State, it is your duty to see that the full quota of troops be constantly kept in the field for the time they have been required. You are responsible to the government; your officer to you. Of what avail is it to give an order if it be never executed and may be disobeyed with impunity? Is it by empty mandates that we can hope to conquer our enemies and save our defence-less frontiers from butchery and devastation? Believe me, my valued friend, there are times when it is highly criminal to shrink from responsibility or scruple about the exercise of our powers. There are times when we must disregard punctilious etiquette, and think only of serving our country. What is really our present situation? The enemy we have been sent to subdue may be said, if we stop at this, to be only exasperated. The commander-in-chief, General Pinckney, who supposes me by this time prepared for renewed operations, has ordered me to advance and form a junction with the Georgia army; and upon the expectation that I will do so are all his arrangements formed for the prosecution of the campaign. Will it do to defeat his plans and jeopardize the safety of the Georgia army? The General Government, too, believe, and have a right to believe, that we have now not less than five thousand men in the heart of the enemy's country, and on this opinion are all their calculations bottomed; and must they all be frustrated, and I become the instrument by which it is done? God forbid!

You advise me to discharge or dismiss from service, until the will of the President can be known, such portion of the militia as have rendered three months' service. This advice astonishes me even more than the former. I have no such discretionary power; and if I had, it would be impolitic and ruinous to exercise it. I believed the militia who were not specially received for a shorter period were engaged for six months, unless the objects of the expedition should be sooner attained; and in this opinion I was greatly strengthened by your letter of the 15th, in which you say, when answering my inquiry upon this subject, 'The militia are detached for six months' service;' nor did I know or suppose you had a different opinion until the arrival of your last letter. This opinion must, I suppose, agreeably to your request, be made known to General Roberts' brigade, and then the consequences are not difficult to be foreseen. Every man belonging to it will abandon me on the 4th of next month; nor shall I have the means of preventing it but by the application of force, which under such circumstances I shall not be at liberty to use. I have laboured hard to reconcile these men to a continuance in service until they could be honourably discharged, and had hoped I had in a great measure succeeded; but your opinion, operating with their own prejudices, will give a sanction to their conduct, and render useless any further attempts. They will go; but I can neither discharge nor dismiss them. Shall I be told that, as they will go, it may as well be peaceably permitted? Can that be any good reason why I should do an unauthorized act? Is it a good reason why I should violate the order of my superior officer and evince a willingness to defeat the purposes of my government? And wherein does the 'sound policy' of the measures that have been recommended consist? or in what way are they 'likely to promote the public good'? Is it sound policy to abandon a conquest thus far made, and deliver up to havoc or add to the number of our enemies those friendly Creeks and Cherokees who, relying on our protection, have espoused our cause and aided us with their arms? What! Retrograde under such circumstances? I will perish first. No. I will do my duty; I will hold the posts I have established, until ordered to abandon them by the commanding general, or die in the struggle; long since have I determined not to seek the preservation of life at the sacrifice of reputation.

But our frontiers, it seems, are to be defended; and by whom? By the very force that is now recommended to be dismissed: for I am first told to retire into the settlements and protect the frontiers; next to discharge my troops; and then that no measures can be taken for raising others. No, my friend, if troops be given me, it is not by loitering on the frontiers that I will seek to give protection: they are to be defended, if defended at all, in a very different manner—by carrying the war into the heart of the enemy's country. All other hopes of defence are more visionary than dreams.

What, then, is to be done? I'll tell you what. You have only to act with the energy and decision the crisis demands, and all will be well. Send me a force engaged for six months and I will answer for the result; but withhold it and all is lost—the reputation of the State, and yours and mine along with it.

Fortunately, Governor Blount had not only the sense to see into what errors he had fallen, when the real state of the case and the obligations it placed upon him were thus pointed out, but the courage also to act inconsistently and to do that which he had once solemnly declared that he ought not to do. It was too late to undo the mischief he had done by advising the discharge of the discontented militia, but he set to work at once to provide men to take their places. The militia left in spite of all that Jackson cared to do to detain them, and Cocke's volunteers followed them ten days afterward, but in the meantime a force of nine hundred new men had arrived. They had enlisted in part for two and in part for three months, and were therefore of comparatively little value; but Jackson resolved to use them at least while waiting for the arrival of the larger and better force which had been ordered to gather at Fayetteville on the 28th of January. He meant to strike a blow with what force he had while its enlistment should continue, so that no more men might be paid for service as soldiers without doing any fighting. The volunteers whose term had expired marched out of camp on the 14th of January, and on the next day Jackson set his new men in motion for work.

They were undrilled, undisciplined, and weak in numbers, but Jackson was now bent upon fighting with anything that he could get which remotely resembled an army.

CHAPTER 27

Battles of Emuckfau
and Enotachopco

In an earlier chapter of this book the author expressed the opinion that if the Creeks could have had an equal share with their enemies in writing the history of the war their story would have given us very different impressions from those that we now have with respect to many of the events of the struggle. Perhaps no better illustration of the truth of this assumption could be given than that which is furnished by the story of Jackson's short campaign with his two and three months' men. The Creek chiefs who fought this force in the battles of Emuckfau and Enotachopco always declared, in talking of the matter after the war, that they "whipped Captain Jackson and ran him to the Coosa River," and while neither Jackson's report of the campaign nor any other of the written accounts of it, admit the truth of this Indian version of the story, they furnish a good many details which strongly suggest that the Creek chiefs may not have been altogether wrong in their interpretation of events.

But as they had no historians to put their account upon record, except by reporting their verbal assertion which we have quoted, the writer is compelled to rely upon the testimony of the other side exclusively for all information about matters of detail.

The force which had come from Tennessee consisted of about nine hundred men in all, of whom eight hundred and fifty were fit for duty. They were in two regiments, one commanded by Colonel Perkins, the other by Colonel Higgins.

With this small force Jackson at once began his march. Crossing the Coosa River on the day after their arrival, he pushed forward to Talladega, where he was reinforced by a body of friendly Indians consisting of sixty-five Cherokees and about two hundred Creeks. He had with him an artillery detachment with a single iron six pounder cannon; a company of spies under Captain Russell, and another under Captain Gordon; and one company composed exclusively of officers. These were officers of various grades whose men had gone home. General Coffee, whose troops also had left him, had gathered these officers together and commanded them in person. General Jackson said in his report that his force numbered exactly nine hundred and thirty men, exclusive of the friendly Indians who accompanied him. These Indians are said to have been somewhat alarmed when they saw how small a force Jackson had with him, but there is nothing to show that they in the least faltered in their duty or hesitated to march when ordered to do so.

General Floyd was already moving to strike the Creeks again, having recovered from his wound. Of this movement and of the nature of Floyd's plans Jackson was advised, in order that he might as far as possible arrange his own in accordance with them.

At Talladega General Jackson received a despatch from Colonel Snodgrass, commanding at Fort Armstrong, that a force of Creeks had assembled at Emuckfau, in a bend of the Tallapoosa River, near the mouth of Emuckfau Creek, in what is now Tallapoosa County, Alabama, and that these Indians, now about nine hundred strong, were preparing to attack Fort Armstrong. Jackson resolved to find and fight this Creek force at once. His men, as he tells us in his report, were both undrilled and insubordinate, and their officers were without skill or experience; but the troops were really anxious to fight a battle, and in this particular their general was disposed to gratify them as speedily as possible. Luckily he had a few good men upon whom he could depend, and his company of brave and experienced officers who were serving as private soldiers with General Coffee for their captain were his special staff of reliance.

Pushing forward as rapidly as possible, the army arrived at Enotachopco, about a dozen miles from Emuckfau, on the afternoon of January 20th. The march was resumed the next morning, and early in the day signs were discovered of the proximity of a large Creek force. Well-beaten trails were found, and a few Indians seen.

It was necessary now to reconnoitre before proceeding further, in order to avoid a surprise in some unfavourable spot. Jackson selected a halting-place and ordered the men to encamp in the form of a hollow square, taking great pains to surround the camp with a line of well-placed picket-guards. Then he sent out his spies to discover the whereabouts and the strength of the Indian force.

Before midnight the spies reported that a large Indian encampment lay within about three miles of Jackson's position, and that the Indians were removing their women and evidently preparing for battle. It was probable that they did not intend to await Jackson's attack, but intended to fall upon his camp during the night, but the careful commander, having already taken every precaution against surprise, contented himself with warning the pickets against neglect of vigilance and the men against panic in the event of a night attack.

The Indians advanced as morning approached, and at six o'clock, while it was not yet light, fell upon Jackson's left flank with great fury. The men, raw as they were, behaved well and met the assault with spirit. General Coffee rode at once to the point at which the firing was heaviest, and both by his presence and his words animated the men; but the struggle was a severe one, and for a time the left flank was so hard pressed that their ability to hold their position was a matter of some doubt. As soon as it was light enough to see, and hence light enough to move troops from one part of the line to another without danger of producing confusion and panic, a fresh company of infantry was ordered to reinforce the left; and Coffee, who with the adjutant-general, Colonel Sitler, and the inspector-general, Colonel Carroll, for his aids, had assumed the immediate command, ordered the whole line forward, leading the men to one of the most gallant and determined charges of the war. Thus assaulted the Creeks gave way, and after a few moments of irregular resistance fled precipitately, closely pressed both by the troops and by the friendly Indians. Coffee with his usual vigour followed the broken and retreating savages for two miles, inflicting considerable damage upon them.

Then Jackson ordered Coffee to take four hundred men and march to the Indian encampment, about three miles away, and, if it should be practicable, to destroy it. He cautioned the gallant, and perhaps too daring general—who was said by one of his contemporaries to have been "a great soldier without knowing it"—to avoid unnecessary risk, and not to attack the place if it should prove upon inspection to be strong.

Coffee marched at once, taking the single piece of artillery with him; but upon arriving at Emuckfau he found the place so well fortified and the force there so strong that he deemed it important not only to withdraw without attacking, but to hasten his return to the camp lest the army thus divided should be attacked and beaten in detail. It was soon made plain that the attack of the morning had been not much more than a beginning of the Indian attempt to overwhelm Jackson.

Half an hour after Coffee returned the Creeks renewed the battle. A considerable force began the action by making an assault upon Jackson's right flank. As soon as their line was developed Coffee asked permission to turn their left flank—moving from the rear of Jackson's right—with two hundred men. Through some misunderstanding only fifty-four men accompanied Coffee, but that particularly enterprising officer, not to be balked of his purpose or delayed in executing it, dashed on though the woods with his little force, which consisted chiefly of his own officer company, and fell upon the flank of the savages fiercely. Jackson, seeing with how small a force Coffee was making this critical movement, moved two hundred friendly Indians to the right to assist the flanking party by attacking that part of the Indian line in front.

Had the Indian attack been what it appeared to be, the battle would have been decided by the results of this combined blow upon the Indian left—from Jackson's right and Coffee's position beyond; but it was presently apparent that the attack upon the right of Jackson's line was merely a feint designed to distract attention from the real object of the savage leader, and to lead Jackson to strengthen his right at the expense of his left, upon which the savages intended then to fall with crushing force.

In this scheme the Indians were baffled. Jackson, anticipating something of the sort, not only avoided weakening his left, but specially commanded the officers there to expect an attack in force and prepare to meet it.

As soon as the right was fully engaged, the main body of the

Indians advanced with spirit and confidence against the left. The assault was well made, the shock falling upon the whole front of the left flank at once; but it was equally well received. For a time the firing was very heavy and at short range; then, knowing that raw troops can stand any amount of active work better than a strain which must be borne passively, Jackson, who had ridden to this part of the field as soon as the alarm was given, ordered his men to cease firing, fix bayonets, charge, and sweep the field. The men behaved, Jackson tells us, with "astonishing intrepidity," and quickly cleared their front, Colonel Carroll leading the charge. The Indians wavered, gave way, and then broke and fled in confusion, under a destructive fire, and with their pursuers close upon their heels.

The friendly Indians did good work whenever actual fighting was going on in their front, but being without that habit of unquestioning obedience which more than any thing else makes the difference between a good soldier and a raw recruit, they could never be depended upon to execute an order the ulterior purpose of which they could not see. In this battle of Emuckfau their habit of acting for the good of the cause upon their own judgment and without regard to orders came near involving Coffee and his company of officers in serious disaster. When Jackson ordered them to the right to co-operate with Coffee, they went gladly and fought well, enabling Coffee to drive the savages in his immediate front into the swamps; but when the firing began on the left they quickly withdrew from the position they had been ordered to occupy, and went to join in the mêlée at the other end of the line, without pausing to think of what might befall Coffee in consequence.

No sooner had they gone than the Creeks rallied and attacked Coffee again, well-nigh overwhelming his small force with their greater numbers. Luckily, Coffee was both an able and an experienced officer, and it was equally a fortunate circumstance that his followers, the ex-officers, were the very best troops in the army, else the whole of the little band, including Coffee, an officer whom Jackson could ill have spared, must have been destroyed. The little band fought with desperate determination, holding their ground and keeping the Indians at bay, but having to fight on every side at once. Coffee fell severely wounded, but continued to direct the operations of his men. His *aide-de-camp* and three others of his followers were killed.

Jackson, hearing the firing on that flank, recalled the friendly Indians from the pursuit at the left as soon as he could, and sent them at double-quick to rescue Coffee. They came up at a run and with a yell, headed by their chief, Jim Fife. As soon as Coffee was thus reinforced he ordered a charge, before which the foe gave way and fled, followed for miles by the relentless Jim Fife and his Indians.

Thus ended the battle of Emuckfau. Whether or not it ended in victory for Jackson is a question with two sides to it, even when the evidence comes to us altogether from one side. Jackson held the field, it is true, but he did not think it prudent to advance a few miles and destroy the Indian encampment. He determined, on the contrary, to retreat without delay to Fort Strother, and even for the single night that he was to remain on the battle-field he deemed it necessary to fortify his camp. Certainly he did not regard the Indians as very badly beaten on this occasion. They were still so dangerously strong that the American commander thought it necessary to provide camp defences, which he had not thought of on the preceding night. In view of these things and of the retreat and pursuit which followed, we may fairly acquit the Indians of the charge of unduly boasting when they said, as already quoted, "We whipped Captain Jackson and ran him to the Coosa River."

In his official report of the affair, Jackson explained his determination to retreat by saying:

Having brought in and buried the dead and dressed the wounded, I ordered my camp to be fortified, to be the better prepared to repel any attack which might be made in the night, determining to make a return march to Fort Strother the following day. Many causes concurred to make such a measure necessary. As I had not set out prepared or with a view to make a permanent establishment, I considered it worse than useless to advance and destroy an empty encampment. I had, indeed, hoped to have met the enemy there; but having met and beaten them a little sooner, I did not think it necessary or prudent to proceed any further—not necessary, because I had accomplished all I could expect to effect by marching to their encampment, and because, if it was proper to contend with and weaken their forces still farther, this object would be more certainly attained by commencing a return, which having to them the appearance of a retreat, would inspirit them to pursue me: not prudent, because of the number of my wounded; of the reinforcements from below, which the enemy might be expected to receive; of the starving condition of my horses, they having had neither corn nor cane for two days and nights; of the scarcity of supplies for my men, the Indians who joined me at Talladega having drawn none and being wholly destitute; and because if the enemy pursued me, as it was likely they would, the diversion in favour of General Floyd would be the more complete and effectual.

The retreat began the next morning, and was conducted with all the caution and care possible. Jackson knew very well that the fight of the day before had been really little better than a drawn battle. He knew that he had not broken the strength of the Indian force which he had been fighting, and that their running away was the running away of Indians, not of regular soldiers; that it indicated no demoralization or loss of readiness to renew the fight, but merely their conviction that for the moment they had better run away. This distinction is an important one to be made. When a disciplined army breaks before the enemy and runs away, the fact proves their utter discomfiture; it shows that they have lost spirit and abandoned their standards in panic, and in such a case it is certain that they are in no fit condition to renew the battle either offensively or defensively. But, in the case of Indians, running away indicates nothing of the kind. Indians fight in a desultory way, advancing and retiring equally without regard to regular principles. They run away if they think that to be the best thing to do for the moment, whether they are frightened or not; and the moment they see an opportunity to strike their foes successfully, they are as ready to turn and fight as they were to run.

Jackson knew this, and hence he made his retreat with all points guarded against surprise. Before nightfall he had reached Enota-chopco, and there he selected a camp with reference to its defensive capabilities, and strongly fortified it before permitting his men to go to rest for the night. The Indians were discovered to be in the neighbourhood, having dogged the retreating army's footsteps through the day, but the precautions taken to strengthen the camp deterred them from attacking during the night.

The next morning, January 24th, Jackson had even greater reason than on the preceding day to anticipate an attack. His pursuers had shown themselves rather boldly during the night, and were evidently contemplating an assault upon his column during the day's march. Knowing that the deep Enotachopco Creek between two hills lay just ahead of him, and that the road by which he was retreating crossed this creek in a defile which offered his pursuers every opportunity to attack him with advantage, Jackson ordered his guides to seek a more favourable place of crossing, and they chose a place where the banks were clear of reeds and underbrush, and where, if attacked, the army could defend itself better than at the regular place of crossing. When the guides reported Jackson moved out of his camp in the order of a harassed general in retreat. He moved in three columns, with strong front and rear guards out, the wounded men in the centre, and light companies on the flanks. He had even taken the precaution, so confident was he that his enemy would attack him that morning, of making his dispositions for battle, issuing a general order instructing the men in what order to form in the event of an attack in front, in rear, or on either flank.

Can we wonder that the Indians who saw all these precautions taken believed that they had "whipped Captain Jackson" and were "driving him to the Coosa River"?

The army moved forward in this cautious way and arrived at the creek. The advance-guard crossed first, and after them the wounded were carried to the opposite shore. Having cared for the helpless wounded men, the solitary gun in the army's possession became the next most important object of solicitude, and the artillery company advanced to cross. Just as they were entering the water a shot in the rear announced that the enemy was pressing Colonel Carroll, who had command there. According to Jackson's orders for the formation of a line of battle in the event of an attack from the rear, Carroll, with the centre column of the rear-guard, was to face about and maintain his position with his front to the rear of the line of march; Colonel Perkins, commanding the right column of the rear-guard, was to face to the right and wheel to the right, using Carroll's flank as a pivot; while Colonel Stump, with the left column of the rear-guard, was to execute a corresponding movement, thus inclosing the enemy's force within three sides of a hollow square, and attacking him simultaneously in front and on both flanks.

Colonel Carroll executed his part of the manoeuvre perfectly. The moment that the savages attacked the rear company in the column, he faced his men about, deployed them in line, and received the shock of the onset manfully; but the right and left columns behaved badly, breaking and fleeing precipitately without firing a gun. The worst of it was that their flight bred a panic among the troops of the centre, and nearly the whole force fled like a mob, Colonel Stump actually leading the retreat, riding frantically into and across the creek. As he passed by Jackson, the infuriated general, who had chosen the ground in the hope that he might crush the enemy here by attacking him on all sides, made an effort to cut the coward down with his sword, but without success.

The flight had effectually dissipated all hopes of winning a victory, and it had done more—it had left the worthy men of the army, very nearly all of them who were worth having in an army at all, exposed to destruction. Colonel Carroll had only twenty-five men left, with Captain Quarles in direct command, but he stood firm and held his ground like a soldier. Jackson says, in his elaborate report:

> There was then left to repulse the enemy the few who remained of the rear-guard, the artillery company, and Captain Russell's company of spies. They, however, realized and exceeded my highest expectations. Lieutenant Armstrong, who commanded the artillery company in the absence of Captain Deadcrick (confined by sickness), ordered them to form and advance to the top of the hill, whilst he and a few others dragged up the six-pounder. Never was more bravery displayed than on this occasion. Amidst the most galling fire from the enemy, more than ten times their number, they ascended the hill, and maintained their position until their piece was hauled up, when having levelled it they poured upon the enemy a fire of grape, reloaded and fired again,

charged and repulsed them. The most deliberate bravery was displayed by Constantine Perkins and Craven Jackson, of the artillery, acting as gunners. In the hurry of the moment, in separating the gun from the limbers, the rammer and picker of the cannon were left tied to the limber. No sooner was this discovered than Jackson, amidst the galling fire of the enemy, pulled out the ramrod of his musket and used it as a picker, primed with a cartridge, and fired the cannon. Perkins, having pulled off his bayonet, used his musket as a rammer and drove down the cartridge; and Jackson, using his former plan, again discharged her. The brave Lieutenant Armstrong, just after the first fire of the cannon, with Captain Hamilton of East Tennessee, Bradford, and McGavock, all fell, the lieutenant exclaiming as he lay, 'My brave fellows, some of you may fall, but you must save the cannon!'

The charge made by the artillery company was seconded by Captain Gordon's spies, who, marching at the head of the column, had crossed the creek when the action began, but who quickly turned and recrossed, striking the enemy in the left flank. A number of other men had now rallied and regained their positions in the line, and as soon as a determined assault was made the enemy gave way and the field was cleared, leaving Jackson free to resume his retreat toward the Coosa River.

In the two battles of Emuckfau and Enotachopco the Indian loss was heavy, one hundred and eighty-nine bodies being found on the field. Jackson's loss was twenty men killed and seventy-five wounded, some of them mortally. Among the killed was Captain Quarles, who fell at the head of his brave twenty-five rear-guardsmen, who checked the enemy and prevented utter disaster from overtaking the army by their courage and coolness.

General Coffee was moving forward on a litter when the battle at Enotachopco began, suffering from the wound he had received at Emuckfau; but when the army broke into a confused and flying mass he mounted his horse in spite of his condition, and to his exertions chiefly Major Eaton attributes the rallying of the men and the ultimate repulse of the enemy.

It became Coffee's duty to write a letter breaking the news

of Captain Donelson's death to his friends, and in that letter, the manuscript of which is preserved in the archives of the Tennessee Historical Society, he says of the ill-luck of the expedition:

> Our great loss has been occasioned by our troops being raw and undisciplined, commanded by officers of the same description. Had I had my old regiment of cavalry I could have driven the enemy wherever I met them, without loss. But speculation had taken them out of the field, and thus we have suffered for them. Their advisers ought to suffer death for their unwarrantable conduct, and I hope our injured citizens will treat them with the contempt they so justly merit.

Jackson had no sooner reached his camp at Fort Strother, than he called Colonels Perkins and Stump to account for their conduct at Enotachopco, preferring charges against them and sending them before a court-martial for trial. The court, upon the evidence submitted, acquitted Colonel Perkins, but found Colonel Stump guilty of the charge of cowardice, and sentenced him to be cashiered.

CHAPTER 28

The Battle of Calebee Creek

We left Floyd retiring upon his base of supplies on the Chatta-hoochee River after the battle of Autosse, suffering from a wound received in that action. After a few weeks of inaction he resumed operations, with the town of Tookabatcha for the objective point of his campaign. Jackson's chief purpose in his expedition to Emuckfau had been to create a diversion in favour of Floyd, and so help to the accomplishment of that general's purpose. In his report of the operations detailed in the last chapter, Jackson, apparently feeling that it was necessary to vindicate the wisdom of the movement, laid special stress upon the fact that his operations had tended thus to assist Floyd. If Floyd had attained the objects of his expedition, this might have been full recompense for Jackson's ill-success; but almost at the very time when the Red Sticks—for that was the term by which the hostile Creeks were called, because Tecumseh had given sticks painted red to all the Creeks who would "take his talk"—almost almost at the very time, we say, when the Red Sticks were "whipping Captain Jackson" at Emuckfau and Enotachopco, they were also "whipping Captain Floyd"—they always called commanders captains—at Calebee Creek, not defeating him in battle, but so hurting him as to compel him to retire and abandon the purpose with which he set out, even more entirely than they had compelled Jackson to abandon his.

Floyd made his advance slowly and cautiously, pausing to establish forts at intervals so that a line of defensive posts should lie like a trail behind him, protecting his line of communications and affording convenient places for the storage and safe keeping of supplies. He began his march with about twelve hundred infantry, four hundred friendly Indians, one cavalry company and his artillery, making a total force of seventeen hundred or eighteen hundred men. It was his purpose to push his column into the Creek country, not rapidly, but resistlessly; so firmly establishing it as to make it, as it were, a permanent wedge of invasion.

When he arrived at a point on Calebee Creek, in what is now Macon County, Alabama, he determined to establish one of his fortified posts upon some high ground there. Here, however, Red Eagle entered his protest against the plans of the Georgia general. Leading a force of Creeks in person, the commander of the Indians was dogging Floyd's footsteps for several days before his arrival at Calebee Creek, but having selected that as the ground on which he would give battle to the whites, the shrewd Indian general adroitly concealed his presence, so handling his force as to keep himself fully informed of Floyd's movements without permitting that officer to know in return that the enemy was near. Floyd took all those precautions which prudence dictates to a commander marching through an enemy's country, but he does not appear to have discovered Red Eagle's presence, or to have expected the attack that was made upon him on the morning of January 27th.

Adopting the tactics which had so often been used against the Indians, Red Eagle moved his men under cover of darkness into position on three sides of Floyd's camp, and fell upon the post by surprise, making his attack simultaneously in front and upon both flanks. In order to effect this surprise, Red Eagle and his men had lain concealed in the swamps until about half after five o'clock in the morning, and then, while it was still entirely dark, made their assault quickly, silently, and so violently as to crowd the sentries back and reach the lines of the camp itself before Floyd's men could form. The troops, thus rudely and suddenly awakened from their slumbers by an attack which does not appear to have been in the least expected, behaved particularly well, forming without confusion and maintaining a firm front in the darkness.

The assault of the savages was fierce and determined. They always fought better under Red Eagle's eye than at other times. Even when Captain Thomas brought his artillery to the front, supported by Captain Adams's riflemen, and opened that fire of grapeshot which Indians have everywhere found it most difficult to stand against, the Red Sticks not only held their ground, but gallantly advanced their line until it was not more than thirty yards distant from the guns, and there, at short pistol range, endured the murderous discharges from the cannon.

The friendly Indians in camp did little during this part of the action, being panic-stricken by the suddenness of the alarm, but the whites everywhere behaved well.

Captain Broadnax, in command of a picket post, was passed by the Indian line at the first assault, and was thus cut off from the camp and the army, but refusing to surrender, he and his squad cut their way through the lines of the enemy and reached their friends in safety.

While darkness lasted Floyd could do nothing more than stand on the defensive. As soon as the light was sufficient to justify an attempt to shift the positions of his battalions, he ordered his right and left wings to swing round to the front upon their pivots, so as to reverse the order of the battle and enclose the Indian force within three sides of a parallelogram. As soon as this movement was executed he ordered a charge, which quickly drove the savages back to the swamps, whither they were pursued by the cavalry, the light companies, and the friendly Indians, who had now recovered their courage.

In the battle Floyd's horse was killed under him. His loss was seventeen white men and five friendly Indians killed, and one hundred and thirty-two white men and fifteen friendly Indians wounded. He was sorely hurt, and it was not known how much damage he had inflicted in return, although it is pretty certain that Floyd had greatly the worst of the affair. He held the battle-field, it is true, but the Indians were manifestly disposed to renew the attack, and for that purpose were still hovering around his camp and threatening it. It was clear that they believed themselves to be the winners in the action, and that they were preparing to renew it and to crush the Georgia army.

Floyd feared they might accomplish this. His respect for Red Eagle's skill as a commander was so increased by the experience of that morning that he abandoned the object for which he had set out, and retreated again.

It is said that Zachariah McGirth—whom the reader will re-member as the half-breed who, supposing that his family were among the victims at Fort Mims, became a despatch-bearer, and dared all manner of dangers—arrived at Floyd's head-quarters on the night of the attack, bearing a despatch from Claiborne. He had passed through the swamp when it was filled with lurking Indians awaiting the moment of attack.

CHAPTER 29

Red Eagle's Strategy

When Red Eagle established his camp at the Holy Ground, from which Claiborne drove him, his purpose was to provide for resistance by concentrating the warriors of the nation after the manner of civilized armies. The Indian practice of breaking into small, roving bands and concentrating only when some special occasion arose, was in favour among the Creek chiefs, but Red Eagle was too capable a soldier not to see how fatal this practice must be in the end. After the massacre at Fort Mims it was his wish to keep his army together and operate with persistent vigour against Mobile if he could gain Spanish consent, and if not, against Georgia and Tennessee. If he could have done this, there can be little doubt that he would have driven Jackson from Fort Strother during the days of starvation and mutiny, by bringing a strong force forward to the attack. His influence had been greatly weakened, however, by his attempt to restrain the demoniac fury of his men at Fort Mims, and in spite of all that he could do, his army dissolved into small wandering bands before he could strike an effective blow. The warriors were still willing enough to serve under his command whenever occasion for an immediate fight should arise, but he could not restrain their natural tendencies, or convert them from their practice of desultory warfare to a policy of systematic operations. Hence Jackson had time for his long struggle with his mutinous men, and escaped the destruction which must otherwise have threatened him for want of an efficient army.

Seeing how impossible it was to convert the savage Creeks into a cohesive body of civilized troops, and to use them as an aggressive army, Red Eagle sought to do the next best thing—namely, to establish strong posts at certain strategic points, collect his warriors around them, and moving out from them, as occasion should offer, strike sudden blows at advancing columns of whites.

In pursuance of this policy he fortified the Holy Ground, from which Claiborne drove him on the 23rd of December, as has been related in a former chapter. The Holy Ground was only one of Red Eagle's strategic points, however. He established the post at Emuckfau, against which Jackson marched with the slender success already described, and a still more important one a few miles away—at Tohopeka, or the Horse Shoe. This Horse Shoe is a peninsula formed by a sharp bend in the Tallapoosa River, enclosing about one hundred acres of ground, high in the middle and marshy along the river-bank. This peninsula, together with an island in the river, Red Eagle selected as the central stronghold of the nation, and he strengthened it by every means in his power. Of that, however, we shall have occasion to speak more fully hereafter; just now we are concerned only with Red Eagle's general disposition of his force.

When Jackson advanced from Fort Strother and Floyd from the Chattahoochee River, the wisdom of the Indian commander's arrangements was made manifest. From his central positions he was able to send five hundred warriors against Jackson; for notwithstanding the assertions frequently made that Jackson was outnumbered at Emuckfau and Enotachopco, it is apparently a well-established fact that the Indian force there was only five hundred strong, while he himself led a larger force against Floyd's larger and better organized army. He was thus able to defeat the plans of both generals, getting the best of both, and compelling both to abandon the objects with which they had set out. He struck them in detail, after the best modes of grand tactics, and his plan of operations bears the test of the soundest military criticism. His first purpose was to strike the two armies separately; his second to interpose his own forces between them, so that if he should be forced back toward the point of convergence of the two lines of march his own divided force would be united before his enemies could form a junction with each other. This was thoroughly good grand tactics; it was precisely the course which any trained military commander in like circumstances would have adopted.

It would perhaps be too much to say that Red Eagle either overcame his two skilled opponents in battle or outgeneralled them in his strategy; but it is not too much to say that he read their purpose, and thwarted them, or that he fairly matched their tactics with his own, and inflicted upon them in battle at least as severe damage as he himself suffered. They outnumbered him in both instances; their men were civilized and organized, while his were savages without organization, discipline, or training; they had artillery to aid them and he had none, many of his men having no better arms than bows and war-clubs; yet he managed so firmly to resist their advance as to turn both of them back in worse condition than they left him. Shall we hesitate to recognize this man as a thoroughly capable military commander, who, with very imperfect means and against tremendous odds, acquitted himself well? It would be idle to speculate upon what Red Eagle might have accomplished if he could have had means equal to those of his enemies; but it is only just to recognize his genius as it was shown in what he did with the inadequate means at his command. He was an Indian and the commander of savages; but he was a patriot, who fought for what he believed to be the interest of his country, and he fought with so much skill and so much courage as to win the admiration and even the friendship of Jackson, whose manly spirit recognized a brother in the not less manly spirit of the Creek chieftain.

Red Eagle's success was necessarily but temporary. It was not in the nature of things that he should win the war, although he might win a campaign. He had matched the Creek Nation against the United States, and the contest was a hopelessly unequal one. For him to overcome one army and drive it back, broken and discouraged, was only to make certain the coming of another army, stronger and larger, against him. He knew this perfectly, and he had known it probably from the beginning. He had never intended to make the unequal match in which he was engaged; he had meant to lend the strength of the whole Creek Nation to an English army of invasion, and as we know had tried to avoid the contest when he learned that it must be fought by a part of the Creeks only, and without the expected assistance from without. Having entered the war, however, he was determined to fight it out, with all his might, to the very end. In order that his resistance might be as determined as possible, and that the whites might be made to pay a high price for their ultimate victory, he was now gathering men from every available quarter, and strengthening his fortified posts, in which he intended to make his last desperate stand. He had persuaded the warriors of the Ocfuske, Hillabee, Oakchoie, Eufaulahatchee, New Yauca, Fishpond, and Hickory Ground towns to join his forces, and they were now at the Horse Shoe. The end of the war was drawing near, but a fierce battle remained to be fought before the power of the Creeks could be broken.

CHAPTER 30

Jackson With an Army at Last

Jackson's long and earnest entreaty for an army with which to carry on the campaign at last produced its desired effect. He who had so long and vainly begged for men, getting only a handful at a time, and getting even them upon terms which made it impossible to use them with full effect, now saw men coming in great numbers from every quarter to fight under his standard. How far this was merely the accumulated result of his successive pleas, and how far the return of the militiamen who had fought at Emuckfau and Enotachopco, bearing with them their general's warm commendation, was influential in behalf of enlistments, it is difficult to determine; but in some way an enthusiasm for Jackson and for the service had sprung up in Tennessee, and the long baffled and weary general at last, saw coming to him an army five thousand strong an army so greatly outnumbering any force which the Creeks could now put into the field, that its coming promised the speedy overthrow of what remained of the Creek power.

Two thousand men came from West Tennessee, two thousand more from the eastern half of that State. Coffee succeeded in gathering together a part of his old brigade, backed by whom he always felt himself to be capable of accomplishing anything, and at the head of these trained and trusted veterans the general who had made himself Jackson's right hand in all difficult enterprises galloped into the camp at Fort Strother, amid the cheers of all the men assembled there.

Better still, if any thing could be better in Jackson's eyes than Coffee's coming with his hard-fighting old brigade, Colonel Williams arrived on the 6th of February with the Thirty-ninth Regiment of regular troops, a body of men six hundred strong, whose example of discipline as regular soldiers was of incalculable advantage in the work of converting volunteers into something better than raw recruits.

As if to verify the adage that "it never rains but it pours," a messenger came from the chiefs of the Choctaw Nation offering the services of all their warriors for the campaign.

Thus at last Jackson had an army as large as he needed or wanted, but before moving such a force it was necessary to provide an abundant supply of food for them, and this was no light task. The winters in North Alabama are rainy, with alternate freezings and thawings, which render roads almost impassable; and in addition to the usual difficulty of securing the food needed there was the still greater difficulty of transporting the supplies from Fort Deposit to Fort Strother to be overcome.

Jackson bent all his energies to this task. He set large forces of his men at work upon the road, paving it in the worst places with logs, making what is called in the South a corduroy road of it. In spite of all that could be done, however, the road remained a bad one, and it was with great difficulty that wagons moved over it at a snail's pace, even when drawn by four horses and very lightly loaded. Seven days were consumed upon each wagon journey from Fort Deposit to the Ten Islands, although a force of men accompanied each wagon to lift it out of mires and hurry it forward. The wagons were lightly loaded too, else they could not have made the journey at all. The strongest of the teams could draw no more than sixteen hundred pounds.

Little by little the supplies were brought up in this laborious fashion, and meantime boats were built, with which Jackson intended to send his provisions down the Coosa River, while he should march his men overland to an appointed place of rendezvous.

At last all was ready. Jackson had a satisfactory army and a satisfactory supply of food for his men, and he was now at last prepared to crush the Creeks by an irresistible blow, delivered at the centre of their strength. There was no chance now for any Creek force to "whip Captain Jackson."

Sending his wounded and sick men to Tennessee, Jackson sent his flatboats down the river, accompanied by the regiment of United States regular troops as a guard. Then, leaving Colonel Steele with a garrison of four hundred men to hold Fort Strother, and if necessary to co-operate with the troops left between that point and Fort Deposit in protecting the army's communications, Jackson began his final march into the Creek Nation, at the head of three thousand effective men.

CHAPTER 31

The Great Battle of the War

The Indians were now concentrated at Tohopeka, or the Horse Shoe, the peninsula already mentioned, which was formed by a sharp bend of the Tallapoosa River, as the reader will see by reference to any good map of Alabama, as the place has not lost its name.

This bend encloses about one hundred acres of ground, and the distance across its neck or narrowest part is between three hundred and four hundred yards. Across this isthmus the Indians had constructed a strong breastwork composed of heavy timbers built up into a thick wall, and designed, unlike the ordinary Indian stockade, to withstand artillery fire. This breastwork was provided with portholes through which the fire of the garrison could be delivered, and the angles of the fortification were so well and so regularly drawn after the manner of educated military engineers, that any force which should approach it in assault must do so at cost of marching under a front and an enfilading fire. Care was taken also so to dispose the houses within the enclosure, the log-heaps, felled trees, and even the earth in some places, as to make additional fortifications of all of them; and about one hundred canoes were fastened along the river-bank as a means of retreat to the forest on the other side in the event of defeat.

All of this systematic preparation, and especially the erecting of the strong and well-placed breastworks, were things wholly new in Indian warfare. This is not the way in which the savage warrior prepares himself for battle: it is the method of the trained soldier; and Mr. Parton, struck with the unlikeness of the preparations to anything ordinarily seen in Indian warfare, says:

As the Indian is not a fortifying creature, it seems improbable that Indians alone were concerned in putting this peninsula into the state of defence in which Jackson found it.

To which we may add, that Red Eagle was not only an Indian chief: he was on one side the white man, William Weatherford, and the white man in him was essentially a civilized white man. He had been trained by that old soldier, General Alexander McGillivray, and by that other soldier, General Le Clerc Milfort; he had visited Mobile and Pensacola, and must have learned both the nature and the elementary principles of fortification there. It was he who planned the establishment of the strongholds of which Tohopeka was one, and what is more probable than that he planned the defences whose fitness for their purpose was so remarkable?

The fighting force of the Creeks at Tohopeka is believed to have been about one thousand strong. They had with them, of course, their women and children, and they had news of Jackson's approach; but notwithstanding the overwhelming numbers opposed to them, they remained in their stronghold determined to await their enemy's attack there, instead of hanging upon his flank after their usual manner, and seeking to surprise him.

The road was long and difficult over which Jackson marched. Rather there was no road, and Jackson had to cut one through an unbroken wilderness, establishing a depot of supplies and garrisoning it before he dared advance to the work he had to do.

Finally, on the morning of March 27th, 1814, the Tennessee commander found himself, after all his toils and harassing difficulties, in front of the enemy he had so long wished to meet in a decisive struggle. He had about two thousand effective men with him, the rest having been left in garrison at the different posts which it was necessary to defend.

Having made himself acquainted with the nature of the ground, he sent General Coffee with a force of seven hundred cavalry and six hundred friendly Indians down the river, with orders to cross two miles below and march up the eastern bank to the bend, where he was directed to occupy a continuous line around the curve, and thus cut off retreat across the river.

Then with the main body of his army and his two light field-

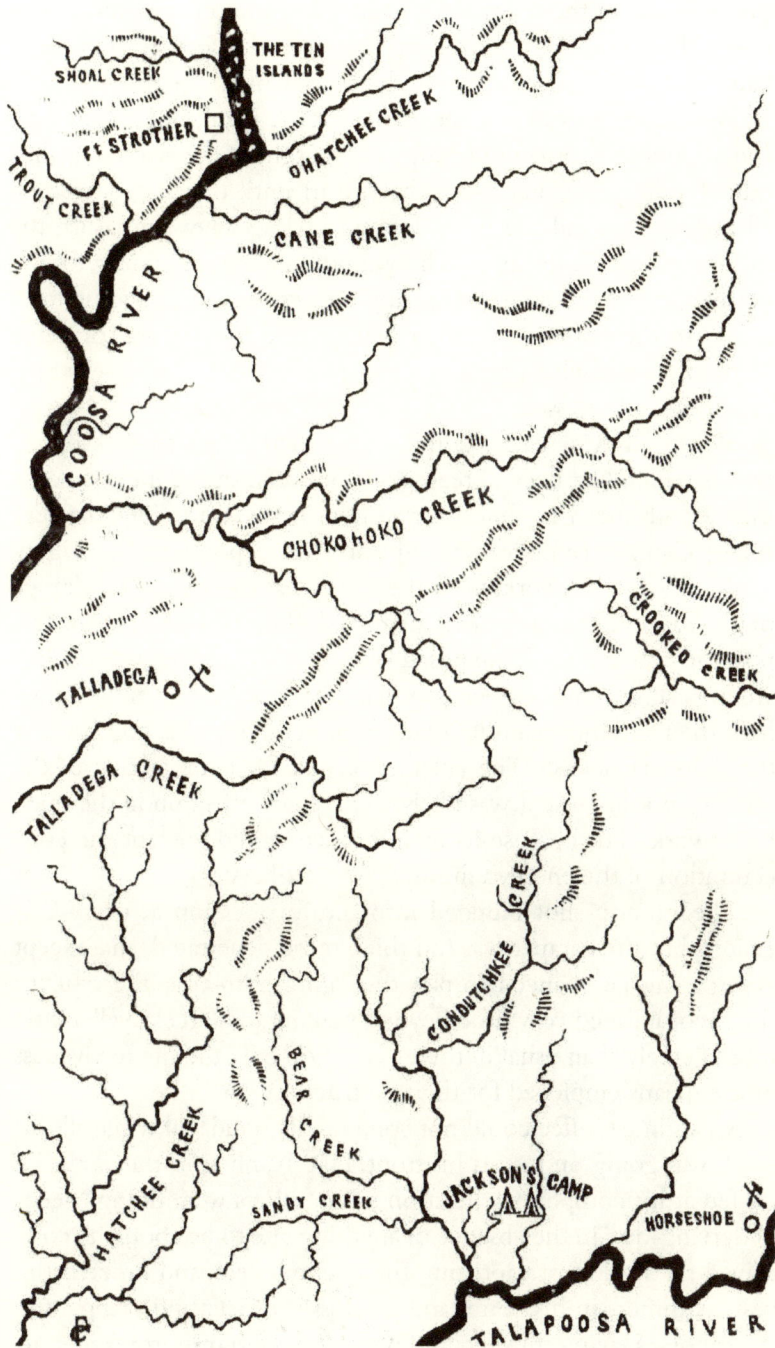

Map of battle site

pieces—one of them a three-pounder and the other a six-pound-er—Jackson himself marched up the river and formed his line of battle across the isthmus, facing the breastworks.

About ten o'clock, Coffee arrived at the bend, and directed his Indians under Morgan to occupy the margin of the river. This they quickly did, deploying along the stream until their line stretched all the way around the bend, leaving no gap anywhere. With the mounted men Coffee posted himself upon a hill just in rear, for the double purpose of intercepting any Creeks who might come from below to the assistance of their beleaguered friends, and of being in position himself to reinforce any part of his Indian line which might be hard pressed.

When all was ready, Coffee signified the fact to Jackson by means which had been agreed upon between them, and the com-mander advanced his line to give the enemy battle. The artillery under Captain Bradford was advanced to a point within eighty yards of the breastwork, with the hope that its fire at short range might make a breach in the formidable line of fortification. The position was a fearfully exposed one for the cannoniers, but they were gallant fellows, under command of a brave officer, and they held their ground manfully under a most galling fire, bombarding the works ceaselessly. The riflemen added their fire to that of the artillery, not because it was likely to have any effect upon the thick breastworks, but because its maintenance would prevent the con-centration of the enemy's fire upon the artillery.

The cannon-shot plunged into the fortification at every dis-charge; but the parapet was too thick to be penetrated, and except when a missile chanced to pass through a port-hole, the artillery fire accomplished very little beyond making the Creeks yell a little more fiercely than usual in their exultation over the ineffectiveness of the means employed for their destruction.

Meantime Coffee could not contentedly stand still while all this work was going on just in his front. Like Ivanhoe in the castle, he chafed at his compulsory inaction while others were doing "deeds of derring-do." In the absence of anything else to be about, he con-ceived the notion of capturing the enemy's fleet, and ordered the best swimmers in his command to cross the river and bring away the canoes. Having thus secured the means of transporting men to the other side, he could not resist the temptation to make an attack in the enemy's rear. If he might have spared enough men for the purpose and led them in person, Coffee would have brought the battle to an early close by this means, saving a deal of bloodshed; but his orders were to maintain a line all along the shore, and to resist the approach of reinforcements from below. He could neither detach a strong force for the attack in rear nor leave his appointed post to lead them in person. But he could at least make a diversion in Jackson's favour, and this he proceeded to do. He sent Morgan across in the canoes, with as many men as could be withdrawn with propriety from the line, ordering him to set fire to the houses by the river-bank and then to advance and attack the savages behind the breastwork.

Morgan executed this order in fine style, and although his force was too small to enable him to maintain his attack for any considerable time, the movement was of great assistance to Jackson. The burning buildings and the crack of Morgan's rifles indicated to Jackson what his active and sagacious lieutenant was doing, and he resolved to seize the opportunity, while the Creeks were somewhat embarrassed by the fire in their rear, to make the direct assault upon the works which it was now evident must be made before any thing effective could be done.

To storm such a work was sure to be a costly way of winning, even if it should succeed, while if it should fail, its failure would mean the utter destruction of the army attempting it. The general hesitated to make so hazardous an attempt, but the men clamoured to be led to the charge. It was the only way, and the army was evidently in the best possible temper for the doing of desperate deeds.

Jackson gave the order to storm the works.

Then was seen the grandest, awfulest thing which war has to show. The long line of men, pressing closely together, advanced with quick, cadenced step, every man knowing that great rents would be made in that line at every second, and none knowing what his own fate might be.

Without wavering, but with compressed lips, the Tennesseeans, in line with Colonel Williams's regulars, rushed upon the breastwork, which flashed fire and poured death among them as they came. Pushing the muzzles of their rifles into the port-holes they delivered their fire, and then clambered up the side of the works, fighting hand to hand with the savages, who battled to beat them back. The first man upon the parapet, Major Montgomery, stood erect but a single second, when he fell dead with a bullet in his brain. His men were close at his heels, and surged like a tide up the slope, pouring in a torrent over the works and into the camp. The breastwork was carried, and in ordinary circumstances the battle would have ended almost immediately in the enemy's surrender; but this enemy had no thought of surrendering. The consequences of a blunder committed so long before as the 18th of November were felt here. General White's attack upon the Hillabees when they had submitted and asked for peace had taught these men to expect nothing but cruellest treachery at the hands of Jackson, whom they confidently believed to be the author of that most unfortunate occurrence. Having no faith in his word, the Creeks believed that he and his men offered quarter only to save themselves the work of killing warriors who could yet fight. They believed that to surrender was only to spare their enemies, who, as soon as the prisoners could be disarmed, would butcher them in cold blood, paying no recompense in the death of any of their own number. Convinced of this, the men at the Horse Shoe simply refused to be taken prisoners, either in a body or singly; they would yield only to death, not to their enemies. They fought for every inch of ground. Wounds were nothing to them, as long as they could level a gun or hurl a tomahawk. Jackson's men had to drive them slowly back, dislodging them from brush heaps and felled trees, and suffering considerable loss in doing so. They had carried the works, but had not yet conquered the defenders of the place. To do that they had simply to butcher them.

It was horrible work, but it must be done. Brave men revolted from it, but whenever one of them sought to spare even a badly-wounded enemy his reward was a bullet, or a blow from the fallen but still defiant warrior's club.

Little by little the savages were driven to the river bank, where the remnant of them made a last stand under strong cover, from which even a well-directed artillery fire at short range failed to dislodge them. They were driven out at last only by the burning of the heap of timber in and behind which they had taken refuge.

When their situation was most desperate, Jackson made a last effort to spare them. Sending a friendly Indian forward, he assured them of his disposition to save them alive if they would surrender, but they answered only by firing upon the messenger and riddling his body with bullets. When at last they were driven out by the flames they were shot down like wild beasts.

Night finally came to stop the slaughter of hiding warriors, but it was renewed in the morning, sixteen warriors being found then concealed in the underbrush. They refused even then to surrender, and were slain.

It was in this battle that Samuel Houston, afterward the president of the Republic of Texas, and still later a Senator in the Congress of the United States, first distinguished himself by his valour, and fell so severely wounded that his recovery was always thought to be little less than miraculous.

When the battle was ended five hundred and fifty-seven dead warriors were found upon the field, but even this was by no means the total number of the slain. Many of them had tried to escape by swimming, and for a long time Coffee's men were busy shooting them in the water, where when killed they sank out of sight.

Mr. Pickett tells us that one brave old chief, Manowa, escaped in an ingenious and wonderful way, after being literally shot to pieces.

> He fought as long as he could. He saved himself by jumping into the river where the water was four feet deep. He held to a root and thus kept himself beneath the waves, breathing through the long joint of a cane, one end of which he held in his mouth, while the other end came above the surface of the water. When night set in the brave Manowa rose from his watery bed and made his way to the forest bleeding from many wounds.

Mr. Pickett conversed with Manowa many years after the war, and heard the story of his escape from his own lips.

Jackson's loss was thirty-two white men and twenty-three friendly Indians killed, ninety-nine white men and forty-seven friendly Indians wounded.

CHAPTER 32

Red Eagle's Surrender

The power of the Creek Nation was crushed at the battle of To-hopeka. The force which fought so desperately there represented not all, but by far the larger part, of what was left of the fighting force of the nation, and they were so utterly beaten that there was nothing to encourage an effort to assemble the scattered warriors again for a struggle. The slight cohesion which tribes of Indians have was gone, and Jackson knew very well that no more severe battles need be fought if the present one was properly followed up with measures designed to convince the Creeks of the uselessness of further resistance. He prepared, therefore, to establish his army in the heart of the Creek Nation, to overawe whatever bands might remain, to strike at roving parties, and to reduce the tribes to submission and peacefulness.

Sinking the bodies of his dead in the river, instead of burying them, he withdrew with his army to Fort Williams, the place he had established and garrisoned as his supply depot, for the double purpose of putting his wounded men into hospital and of replenishing his supply of food, for he had carried nothing with him beyond Fort Williams except one week's provisions in the men's haversacks.

After a tedious march lasting five days, Jackson rested his worn-out men at Fort Williams, and there wrote the following address, which was ordered to be read to the army:

You have entitled yourselves to the gratitude of your country and your general. The expedition from which you have just returned has, by your good conduct, been rendered prosperous beyond any example in the history of our warfare; it has redeemed the character of your State, and of that description of troops of which the greater part of you are.

You have, within a few days, opened your way to the Tallapoosa, and destroyed a confederacy of the enemy, ferocious by nature and who had grown insolent from impunity. Relying on their numbers, the security of their situation, and the assurances of their prophets, they derided our approach, and already exulted in anticipation of the victory they expected to obtain. But they were ignorant of the influence and effect of government on the human powers, nor knew what brave men and civilized could effect. By their yells they hoped to frighten us, and with their wooden fortifications to oppose us. Stupid mortals! Their yells but designated their situation the more certainly, while their walls became a snare for their own destruction. So will it ever be when presumption and ignorance contend against bravery and prudence.

The fiends of the Tallapoosa will no longer murder our women and children, or disturb the quiet of our borders. Their midnight flambeaux will no more illumine their council-house or shine upon the victim of their infernal orgies. In their places a new generation will arise who will know their duty better. The weapons of warfare will be exchanged for the utensils of husbandry; and the wilderness, which now withers in sterility and mourns the desolation which overspreads her, will blossom as the rose and become the nursery of the arts. But before this happy day can arrive other chastisements remain to be inflicted. It is indeed lamentable that the path to peace should lead through blood and over the bodies of the slain; but it is a dispensation of Providence, and perhaps a wise one, to inflict partial evils, that ultimate good may be produced.

Our enemies are not sufficiently humbled; they do not sue for peace. A collection of them await our approach, and remain to be dispersed. Buried in ignorance, and seduced by the false pretences of their prophets, they have the weakness to believe they will still be able to make a decided stand against us. They must be undeceived, and made to atone their obstinacy and their crimes by still further suffering. Those hopes which have so long deluded them must be driven from their last refuge. They must be made to know that their prophets are impostors, and that our strength is mighty and will prevail. Then, and not till then, may we expect to make with them a peace that shall be permanent.

Ten days after the battle of the Horse Shoe the army again advanced, the men carrying provisions in their haversacks as before. A long march brought them to the confluence of the Coosa and Tallapoosa rivers, where a junction with the southern army was effected and supplies were abundant.

There Jackson established his camp and fortified it. The force of Creeks which he had expected to strike had dispersed, and there was now nowhere a body of Indians for him to march against or fight. His presence with a strong army, well supplied with food and able to maintain itself there in the very heart of the nation, did the rest. Seeing the utter hopelessness of contending further with such an army so commanded, and hearing through friendly Indians, who were sent out for the purpose, that Jackson wished to make peace, the savages rapidly flocked to his camp and surrendered themselves.

Peter McQueen, Josiah Francis, and several other chiefs fled to Florida, but the greater number of the Creek leaders preferred to sue for Jackson's clemency.

To them Jackson replied that he had no further desire to make war, but that peace would not be granted to the nation until Red Eagle—or Weatherford, for by that name only the whites called the Creek commander—should be brought to him bound hand and foot. It was his purpose to hang Red Eagle as a punishment for the massacre of women and children at Fort Mims, he knowing nothing, of course, of the warrior's daring efforts to prevent that bloody butchery, and to make of the affair a battle, not a massacre.

News of Jackson's determination was carried to Red Eagle, and he was warned to fly the country and make his escape to Florida, as many of his companion chiefs had done. There, of course, he would have been safe beyond the jurisdiction of Jackson and of the government which Jackson represented; but Red Eagle was a patriot, and when he was told that the fierce commander of the whites would give no terms to the Creeks under which the women and children now starving in the woods could be saved, except upon his surrender, that the price of peace for his people was his own ignominious death—he calmly resolved to give himself to suffer for his race, to purchase with his blood that peace which alone could save his people from destruction.

Mounting his famous gray horse—the one which had carried him over the bluff at the Holy Ground, he rode away alone toward Jackson's camp.

The author of that history of Alabama which has been quoted frequently in these pages gives the following account of what followed, drawn, he assures us, from Red Eagle's own narrative in conversations had with him:

He rode within a few miles of Fort Jackson, when a fine deer crossed his path and stopped within shooting distance, which he fired at and killed. Reloading his rifle with two balls, for the purpose of shooting the Big Warrior, should he give him any cause, at the fort, he placed the deer behind his saddle and advanced to the American outposts. Some soldiers, of whom he politely inquired for Jackson's whereabouts, gave him some unsatisfactory and rude replies, when a gray-headed man a few steps beyond pointed him to the marquee. Weatherford rode up to it and checked his horse immediately at the entrance, where sat the Big Warrior, who exultingly exclaimed:

'Ah! Bill Weatherford, have we got you at last?'

The fearless chieftain cast his keen eyes at the Big Warrior, and said in a determined tone:

'You—traitor, if you give me any insolence I will blow a ball through your cowardly heart.'

General Jackson now came running out of the marquee with Colonel Hawkins, and in a furious manner exclaimed:

'How dare you, sir, to ride up to my tent after having murdered the women and children at Fort Mims?'

Weatherford said:

'General Jackson, I am not afraid of you. I fear no man, for I am a Creek warrior. I have nothing to request in behalf of myself; you can kill me if you desire. But I come to beg you to send for the women and children of the war party, who are now starving in the woods. Their fields and cribs have been destroyed by your people, who have driven them to the woods without an ear of corn. I hope that you will send out parties who will safely conduct them here, in order that they may be fed. I exerted myself in vain to prevent the massacre of the women and children at Fort Mims. I am now done fighting. The Red Sticks are nearly all killed. If I could fight you any longer I would most heartily do so. Send for the women and children. They never did you any harm. But kill me, if the white people want it done.'

At the conclusion of these words many persons who had surrounded the marquee exclaimed:

'Kill him! kill him! kill him!'

General Jackson commanded silence, and in an emphatic manner said:

'Any man who would kill as brave a man as this would rob the dead!'

He then invited Weatherford to alight, drank a glass of brandy with him, and entered into a cheerful conversation under his hospitable marquee. Weatherford gave him the deer, and they were then good friends.

Mr. Pickett discredits the accounts of this affair which were given by persons who were present at its occurrence, but they have been accepted by so many writers of repute, including Eaton and Meek, whose opportunities for learning the truth were as good as his, that Mr. Parton regards them as trustworthy at least in their main features. Following him in this, we give the remainder of the conversation between Jackson and the heroic chieftain. Jackson told Weatherford what terms he had offered to the Creeks, and added:

As for yourself, if you do not like the terms, no advantage shall be taken of your present surrender. You are at liberty to depart and resume hostilities when you please. But, if you are taken then, your life shall pay the forfeit of your crimes.

Straightening himself up, the bold warrior answered:

I desire peace for no selfish reasons, but that my nation may be relieved from their sufferings; for, independent of the other consequences of the war, their cattle are destroyed and their women and children destitute of provisions. But I may well be addressed in such language now. There was a time when I had a choice and could have answered you. I have none now. Even hope has ended. Once I could animate my warriors to battle. But I cannot animate the dead. My warriors can no longer hear my voice. Their bones are at Talladega, Tallushatchee, Emuckfau, and Tohopeka. I have not surrendered myself thoughtlessly. While there were chances of success I never left my post nor supplicated peace. But my people are gone, and I now ask peace for my nation and myself. On the miseries and misfortunes brought upon my country I look back with the deepest sorrow, and wish to avert still greater calamities. If I had been left to contend with the Georgia army I would have raised my corn on one bank of the river, and fought them on the other. But your people have destroyed my nation. General Jackson, you are a brave man; I am another. I do not fear to die. But I rely upon your generosity. You will exact no terms of a conquered and helpless people but those to which they should accede. Whatever they may be, it would now be folly and madness to oppose them. If they are opposed, you shall find me among the sternest enforcers of obedience. Those who would still hold out can only be influenced by a mean spirit of revenge. To this they must not and shall not sacrifice the last remnant of their country. You have told us what we may do and be safe. Yours is a good talk, and my nation ought to listen to it. They shall listen to it.

Jackson was too brave a man not to discover the hero in this courageous, self-sacrificing man, who, knowing that an ignominious death had been determined upon for him, calmly refused to save himself, and boldly placed his life in his enemy's hands for the sake of his people. When two men so brave as these meet there is fellowship between them, because there is brotherhood between their souls. When Red Eagle thus faced Jackson and offered to accept death at his hands in return for peace for the now helpless

Creeks there was peace between the two great-souled men, who knew each other by the free-masonry of a common heroism, a common courage, and a common spirit of self-sacrifice.

Seeing Weatherford in this transaction, do we need to remember his battles as proof that he was a great man in the larger and better sense of the word; that he did his duty, as he understood it, without regard to his personal welfare; that he was a patriot as well as a soldier?

CHAPTER 33

Red Eagle After the War

Having made peace with Red Eagle, Jackson afforded him that protection which was necessary while he was in a camp filled with the friendly Indians, whose hatred of the warrior was undying. Big Warrior even tried to take his life in spite of Jackson's orders, and was restrained only by the general's personal interference.

Red Eagle busied himself at once in the pacification of the country, as he had assured Jackson that he would do, and to his great influence, in a large measure, the prompt acquiescence of the Creeks in the terms of peace was due.

As soon as the country was pacified Red Eagle sought to return to the ways of peace, and for that purpose went to his plantation near Fort Mims, and tried to gather together his property which had become scattered, and resume his business as a planter.

He was not long in learning, however, that his foes among the half-breeds and Indians who had sided with the whites were implacable, and that their thirst for his blood made his peaceful stay there impossible. He therefore went to Fort Claiborne and put himself under the protection of the commanding officer there, who assigned him a tent near his own and a body-guard for his protection. Here Weatherford remained for ten or fifteen days, but there were so many persons in the camp who had lost friends at Fort Mims, and who were determined to take the Creek chieftain's life, that his protector feared to keep him at the fort longer, even under the constant protection of a strong guard detail. But it was dangerous to remove him, except secretly, so determined was the enmity of the men who sought to kill him; and therefore the commander of the post ordered an *aide-de-camp* at midnight to take the great chieftain beyond the camp lines and there to arrange for his escape, through Captain Laval, who was instructed to escort him to a tree outside of the line of outposts. There a powerful horse had been provided, and Red Eagle, mounting the animal, galloped away in the darkness.

Upon his arrival at Jackson's camp he was received by the Tennessee general with the respect due to so gallant a soldier, and there he remained under Jackson's watchful care until after the signing of the treaty of August 9th, 1814, by which the Creeks gave up all the southern part of their territory. This was exacted nominally as an indemnity to the government for the expenses of the war, but the real purpose was to plant a strong and continuous line of white settlements between the Creeks and their bad advisers, the Spanish, at Pensacola. By these means Jackson, who managed the affair, made impossible any future renewal of the war to which he had put an end by arms.

When the treaty was concluded, Jackson's mission was done, and he returned to his Tennessee home—the Hermitage—taking Red Eagle with him as his guest, and in order that the chieftain might be safe from the assassination with which he was still threatened, Jackson carefully concealed the fact of his presence. For nearly a year the two commanders who had fought each other so fiercely lived together as friends under one roof, the conquered the guest of the conqueror.

Then Weatherford returned to Alabama and established himself as a planter. His relatives had saved much of his property, which they returned to him, and by wise management he recovered his fortunes and became again a man of considerable wealth.

His influence was always on the side of law and order, and how valuable the influence of such a man, so exerted, is in a new country, where two races are constantly brought into contact, we may easily conceive.

Red Eagle had been overcome in war, and was disposed to maintain the peace, in accordance with his promise; but his spirit was not broken, and none of his courage had gone out of him.

On one occasion a very brutal assassination was committed at a public sale by two ruffians of the most desperate border type. A magistrate summoned the people as a *posse comitatus* to arrest the offenders, but they so violently swore that they would kill anyone who should approach them, that no man dared attempt the duty. Red Eagle, who was present, expressed his indignation at the murder, and his contempt for the fears of the bystanders, and volunteered to make the arrest if ordered by the magistrate to do so.

The magistrate gave the order, and drawing a long, silver-handled knife, which was his only weapon, Weatherford advanced upon the murderers, who warned him off, swearing that they would kill him if he should advance. Without a sign of hesitation, and with a calm look of resolution in his countenance which appalled even his desperate antagonists, he stepped quickly up to one of them and seized him by the throat, calling to the bystanders to "tie the rascal." Then going up to the other he arrested him, the desperado saying as he approached: "I will not resist you, Billy Weatherford."

Weatherford's plantation was among the white settlements, and the country round about him rapidly filled up with white people, among whom the warrior lived in peace and friendship. Mr. Meek writes of him at this time in these words:

The character of the man seemed to have been changed by the war. He was no longer cruel, vindictive, idle, intemperate, or fond of display: but surrounded by his family he preserved a dignified and retiring demeanour; was industrious, sober, and economical; and was a kind and indulgent master to his servants, of whom he had many. A gentleman who had favourable opportunities of judging says of him that 'in his intercourse with the whites his bearing was marked by nobleness of purpose, and his conduct was always honourable. No man was more fastidious in complying with his engagements. His word was by him held to be more sacred than the most binding legal obligation. Art and dissimulation formed no part of his character. Ever frank and guileless, no one had the more entire confidence of those among whom he lived.' Another gentleman who knew Weatherford intimately for a number of years informs me that 'he possessed remarkable intellectual powers; that his perceptions were quick almost to intuition, his memory tenacious, his imagination vivid, his judgment strong and accurate, and his language copious, fluent, and expressive. In short,' he says, 'Weatherford possessed

naturally one of the finest minds our country has produced.'
These traits of character exhibited for a number of years
won for their possessor the esteem and respect of those who
knew him, notwithstanding the circumstances of his earlier
life. Indeed those circumstances threw around the man a romance of character which made him the more attractive.
After the bitterness which the war engendered had subsided
his narratives were listened to with interest and curiosity.
Though unwilling generally to speak of his adventures, he
would, when his confidence was obtained, describe them
with a graphic particularity and colouring which gave an in-
sight into conditions of life and phases of character of which
we can now only see the outside. He always extenuated his
conduct at Fort Mims and during the war under the plea
that the first transgressions were committed by the white
people, and that he was fighting for the liberties of his nation.
He also asserted that he was reluctantly forced into the war.

Red Eagle died on the 9th of March, 1824, from over-fatigue
incurred in a bear hunt. He left a large family of children, who
intermarried with the whites, well-nigh extinguishing all traces of
Indian blood in his descendants.

LEONAUR

ALSO FROM LEONAUR
AVAILABLE IN SOFTCOVER OR HARDCOVER WITH DUST JACKET

A HISTORY OF THE FRENCH & INDIAN WAR *by Arthur G. Bradley*—The Seven Years War as it was fought in the New World has always fascinated students of military history—here is the story of that confrontation.

WASHINGTON'S EARLY CAMPAIGNS *by James Hadden*—The French Post Expedition, Great Meadows and Braddock's Defeat—including Braddock's Orderly Books.

BOUQUET & THE OHIO INDIAN WAR *by Cyrus Cort & William Smith*—Two Accounts of the Campaigns of 1763-1764: Bouquet's Campaigns by Cyrus Cort & The History of Bouquet's Expeditions by William Smith.

NARRATIVES OF THE FRENCH & INDIAN WAR: 2 *by David Holden, Samuel Jenks, Lemuel Lyon, Mary Cochrane Rogers & Henry T. Blake*—Contains The Diary of Sergeant David Holden, Captain Samuel Jenks' Journal, The Journal of Lemuel Lyon, Journal of a French Officer at the Siege of Quebec, A Battle Fought on Snowshoes & The Battle of Lake George.

NARRATIVES OF THE FRENCH & INDIAN WAR *by Brown, Eastburn, Hawks & Putnam*—Ranger Brown's Narrative, The Adventures of Robert Eastburn, The Journal of Rufus Putnam—Provincial Infantry & Orderly Book and Journal of Major John Hawks on the Ticonderoga-Crown Point Campaign.

THE 7TH (QUEEN'S OWN) HUSSARS: Volume 1—1688-1792 *by C. R. B. Barrett*—As Dragoons During the Flanders Campaign, War of the Austrian Succession and the Seven Years War.

INDIA'S FREE LANCES *by H. G. Keene*—European Mercenary Commanders in Hindustan 1770-1820.

THE BENGAL EUROPEAN REGIMENT *by P. R. Innes*—An Elite Regiment of the Honourable East India Company 1756-1858.

MUSKET & TOMAHAWK *by Francis Parkman*—A Military History of the French & Indian War, 1753-1760.

THE BLACK WATCH AT TICONDEROGA *by Frederick B. Richards*—Campaigns in the French & Indian War.

QUEEN'S RANGERS *by Frederick B. Richards*—John Simcoe and his Rangers During the Revolutionary War for America.

AVAILABLE ONLINE AT www.leonaur.com
AND FROM ALL GOOD BOOK STORES
07/09

LEONAUR

ALSO FROM LEONAUR
AVAILABLE IN SOFTCOVER OR HARDCOVER WITH DUST JACKET

JOURNALS OF ROBERT ROGERS OF THE RANGERS *by Robert Rogers*—The exploits of Rogers & the Rangers in his own words during 1755-1761 in the French & Indian War.

GALLOPING GUNS *by James Young*—The Experiences of an Officer of the Bengal Horse Artillery During the Second Maratha War 1804-1805.

GORDON *by Demetrius Charles Boulger*—The Career of Gordon of Khartoum.

THE BATTLE OF NEW ORLEANS *by Zachary F. Smith*—The final major engagement of the War of 1812.

THE TWO WARS OF MRS DUBERLY *by Frances Isabella Duberly*—An Intrepid Victorian Lady's Experience of the Crimea and Indian Mutiny.

WITH THE GUARDS' BRIGADE DURING THE BOER WAR *by Edward P. Lowry*—On Campaign from Bloemfontein to Koomati Poort and Back.

THE REBELLIOUS DUCHESS *by Paul F. S. Dermoncourt*—The Adventures of the Duchess of Berri and Her Attempt to Overthrow French Monarchy.

MEN OF THE MUTINY *by John Tulloch Nash & Henry Metcalfe*—Two Accounts of the Great Indian Mutiny of 1857: Fighting with the Bengal Yeomanry Cavalry & Private Metcalfe at Lucknow.

CAMPAIGN IN THE CRIMEA *by George Shuldham Peard*—The Recollections of an Officer of the 20th Regiment of Foot.

WITHIN SEBASTOPOL *by K. Hodasevich*—A Narrative of the Campaign in the Crimea, and of the Events of the Siege.

WITH THE CAVALRY TO AFGHANISTAN *by William Taylor*—The Experiences of a Trooper of H. M. 4th Light Dragoons During the First Afghan War.

THE CAWNPORE MAN *by Mowbray Thompson*—A First Hand Account of the Siege and Massacre During the Indian Mutiny By One of Four Survivors.

BRIGADE COMMANDER: AFGHANISTAN *by Henry Brooke*—The Journal of the Commander of the 2nd Infantry Brigade, Kandahar Field Force During the Second Afghan War.

BANCROFT OF THE BENGAL HORSE ARTILLERY *by N. W. Bancroft*—An Account of the First Sikh War 1845-1846.

AVAILABLE ONLINE AT **www.leonaur.com**
AND FROM ALL GOOD BOOK STORES
07/09

LEONAUR

ALSO FROM LEONAUR
AVAILABLE IN SOFTCOVER OR HARDCOVER WITH DUST JACKET

AFGHANISTAN: THE BELEAGUERED BRIGADE *by G. R. Gleig*—An Account of Sale's Brigade During the First Afghan War.

IN THE RANKS OF THE C. I. V *by Erskine Childers*—With the City Imperial Volunteer Battery (Honourable Artillery Company) in the Second Boer War.

THE BENGAL NATIVE ARMY *by F. G. Cardew*—An Invaluable Reference Resource.

THE 7TH (QUEEN'S OWN) HUSSARS: Volume 4—1688-1914 *by C. R. B. Barrett*—Uniforms, Equipment, Weapons, Traditions, the Services of Notable Officers and Men & the Appendices to All Volumes—Volume 4: 1688-1914.

THE SWORD OF THE CROWN *by Eric W. Sheppard*—A History of the British Army to 1914.

THE 7TH (QUEEN'S OWN) HUSSARS: Volume 3—1818-1914 *by C. R. B. Barrett*—On Campaign During the Canadian Rebellion, the Indian Mutiny, the Sudan, Matabeleland, Mashonaland and the Boer War Volume 3: 1818-1914.

THE KHARTOUM CAMPAIGN *by Bennet Burleigh*—A Special Correspondent's View of the Reconquest of the Sudan by British and Egyptian Forces under Kitchener—1898.

EL PUCHERO *by Richard McSherry*—The Letters of a Surgeon of Volunteers During Scott's Campaign of the American-Mexican War 1847-1848.

RIFLEMAN SAHIB *by E. Maude*—The Recollections of an Officer of the Bombay Rifles During the Southern Mahratta Campaign, Second Sikh War, Persian Campaign and Indian Mutiny.

THE KING'S HUSSAR *by Edwin Mole*—The Recollections of a 14th (King's) Hussar During the Victorian Era.

JOHN COMPANY'S CAVALRYMAN *by William Johnson*—The Experiences of a British Soldier in the Crimea, the Persian Campaign and the Indian Mutiny.

COLENSO & DURNFORD'S ZULU WAR *by Frances E. Colenso & Edward Durnford*—The first and possibly the most important history of the Zulu War.

U. S. DRAGOON *by Samuel E. Chamberlain*—Experiences in the Mexican War 1846-48 and on the South Western Frontier.

AVAILABLE ONLINE AT www.leonaur.com
AND FROM ALL GOOD BOOK STORES

07/09

LEONAUR

ALSO FROM LEONAUR

AVAILABLE IN SOFTCOVER OR HARDCOVER WITH DUST JACKET

THE 2ND MAORI WAR: 1860-1861 *by Robert Carey*—The Second Maori War, or First Taranaki War, one more bloody instalment of the conflicts between European settlers and the indigenous Maori people.

A JOURNAL OF THE SECOND SIKH WAR *by Daniel A. Sandford*—The Experiences of an Ensign of the 2nd Bengal European Regiment During the Campaign in the Punjab, India, 1848-49.

THE LIGHT INFANTRY OFFICER *by John H. Cooke*—The Experiences of an Officer of the 43rd Light Infantry in America During the War of 1812.

BUSHVELDT CARBINEERS *by George Witton*—The War Against the Boers in South Africa and the 'Breaker' Morant Incident.

LAKE'S CAMPAIGNS IN INDIA *by Hugh Pearse*—The Second Anglo Maratha War, 1803-1807.

BRITAIN IN AFGHANISTAN 1: THE FIRST AFGHAN WAR 1839-42 *by Archibald Forbes*—From invasion to destruction-a British military disaster.

BRITAIN IN AFGHANISTAN 2: THE SECOND AFGHAN WAR 1878-80 *by Archibald Forbes*—This is the history of the Second Afghan War-another episode of British military history typified by savagery, massacre, siege and battles.

UP AMONG THE PANDIES *by Vivian Dering Majendie*—Experiences of a British Officer on Campaign During the Indian Mutiny, 1857-1858.

MUTINY: 1857 *by James Humphries*—Authentic Voices from the Indian Mutiny-First Hand Accounts of Battles, Sieges and Personal Hardships.

BLOW THE BUGLE, DRAW THE SWORD *by W. H. G. Kingston*—The Wars, Campaigns, Regiments and Soldiers of the British & Indian Armies During the Victorian Era, 1839-1898.

WAR BEYOND THE DRAGON PAGODA *by Major J. J. Snodgrass*—A Personal Narrative of the First Anglo-Burmese War 1824 - 1826.

THE HERO OF ALIWAL *by James Humphries*—The Campaigns of Sir Harry Smith in India, 1843-1846, During the Gwalior War & the First Sikh War.

ALL FOR A SHILLING A DAY *by Donald F. Featherstone*—The story of H.M. 16th, the Queen's Lancers During the first Sikh War 1845-1846.

AVAILABLE ONLINE AT www.leonaur.com
AND FROM ALL GOOD BOOK STORES

07/09

LEONAUR

ALSO FROM LEONAUR
AVAILABLE IN SOFTCOVER OR HARDCOVER WITH DUST JACKET

THE FALL OF THE MOGHUL EMPIRE OF HINDUSTAN *by H. G. Keene*—By the beginning of the nineteenth century, as British and Indian armies under Lake and Wellesley dominated the scene, a little over half a century of conflict brought the Moghul Empire to its knees.

LADY SALE'S AFGHANISTAN *by Florentia Sale*—An Indomitable Victorian Lady's Account of the Retreat from Kabul During the First Afghan War.

THE CAMPAIGN OF MAGENTA AND SOLFERINO 1859 *by Harold Carmichael Wylly*—The Decisive Conflict for the Unification of Italy.

FRENCH'S CAVALRY CAMPAIGN *by J. G. Maydon*—A Special Correspondent's View of British Army Mounted Troops During the Boer War.

CAVALRY AT WATERLOO *by Sir Evelyn Wood*—British Mounted Troops During the Campaign of 1815.

THE SUBALTERN *by George Robert Gleig*—The Experiences of an Officer of the 85th Light Infantry During the Peninsular War.

NAPOLEON AT BAY, 1814 *by F. Loraine Petre*—The Campaigns to the Fall of the First Empire.

NAPOLEON AND THE CAMPAIGN OF 1806 *by Colonel Vachée*—The Napoleonic Method of Organisation and Command to the Battles of Jena & Auerstädt.

THE COMPLETE ADVENTURES IN THE CONNAUGHT RANGERS *by William Grattan*—The 88th Regiment during the Napoleonic Wars by a Serving Officer.

BUGLER AND OFFICER OF THE RIFLES *by William Green & Harry Smith*—With the 95th (Rifles) during the Peninsular & Waterloo Campaigns of the Napoleonic Wars.

NAPOLEONIC WAR STORIES *by Sir Arthur Quiller-Couch*—Tales of soldiers, spies, battles & sieges from the Peninsular & Waterloo campaigns.

CAPTAIN OF THE 95TH (RIFLES) *by Jonathan Leach*—An officer of Wellington's sharpshooters during the Peninsular, South of France and Waterloo campaigns of the Napoleonic wars.

RIFLEMAN COSTELLO *by Edward Costello*—The adventures of a soldier of the 95th (Rifles) in the Peninsular & Waterloo Campaigns of the Napoleonic wars.

AVAILABLE ONLINE AT **www.leonaur.com**
AND FROM ALL GOOD BOOK STORES

07/09

LEONAUR

ALSO FROM LEONAUR
AVAILABLE IN SOFTCOVER OR HARDCOVER WITH DUST JACKET

AT THEM WITH THE BAYONET by *Donald F. Featherstone*—The first Anglo-Sikh War 1845-1846.

STEPHEN CRANE'S BATTLES by *Stephen Crane*—Nine Decisive Battles Recounted by the Author of 'The Red Badge of Courage'.

THE GURKHA WAR by *H. T. Prinsep*—The Anglo-Nepalese Conflict in North East India 1814-1816.

FIRE & BLOOD by *G. R. Gleig*—The burning of Washington & the battle of New Orleans, 1814, through the eyes of a young British soldier.

SOUND ADVANCE! by *Joseph Anderson*—Experiences of an officer of HM 50th regiment in Australia, Burma & the Gwalior war.

THE CAMPAIGN OF THE INDUS by *Thomas Holdsworth*—Experiences of a British Officer of the 2nd (Queen's Royal) Regiment in the Campaign to Place Shah Shuja on the Throne of Afghanistan 1838 - 1840.

WITH THE MADRAS EUROPEAN REGIMENT IN BURMA by *John Butler*—The Experiences of an Officer of the Honourable East India Company's Army During the First Anglo-Burmese War 1824 - 1826.

IN ZULULAND WITH THE BRITISH ARMY by *Charles L. Norris-Newman*—The Anglo-Zulu war of 1879 through the first-hand experiences of a special correspondent.

BESIEGED IN LUCKNOW by *Martin Richard Gubbins*—The first Anglo-Sikh War 1845-1846.

A TIGER ON HORSEBACK by *L. March Phillips*—The Experiences of a Trooper & Officer of Rimington's Guides - The Tigers - during the Anglo-Boer war 1899 - 1902.

SEPOYS, SIEGE & STORM by *Charles John Griffiths*—The Experiences of a young officer of H.M.'s 61st Regiment at Ferozepore, Delhi ridge and at the fall of Delhi during the Indian mutiny 1857.

CAMPAIGNING IN ZULULAND by *W. E. Montague*—Experiences on campaign during the Zulu war of 1879 with the 94th Regiment.

THE STORY OF THE GUIDES by *G.J. Younghusband*—The Exploits of the Soldiers of the famous Indian Army Regiment from the northwest frontier 1847 - 1900.

AVAILABLE ONLINE AT www.leonaur.com
AND FROM ALL GOOD BOOK STORES

07/09

![LEONAUR]

ALSO FROM LEONAUR
AVAILABLE IN SOFTCOVER OR HARDCOVER WITH DUST JACKET

ZULU:1879 *by D.C.F. Moodie & the Leonaur Editors*—The Anglo-Zulu War of 1879 from contemporary sources: First Hand Accounts, Interviews, Dispatches, Official Documents & Newspaper Reports.

THE RED DRAGOON *by W.J. Adams*—With the 7th Dragoon Guards in the Cape of Good Hope against the Boers & the Kaffir tribes during the 'war of the axe' 1843-48'.

THE RECOLLECTIONS OF SKINNER OF SKINNER'S HORSE *by James Skinner*—James Skinner and his 'Yellow Boys' Irregular cavalry in the wars of India between the British, Mahratta, Rajput, Mogul, Sikh & Pindarree Forces.

A CAVALRY OFFICER DURING THE SEPOY REVOLT *by A. R. D. Mackenzie*—Experiences with the 3rd Bengal Light Cavalry, the Guides and Sikh Irregular Cavalry from the outbreak to Delhi and Lucknow.

A NORFOLK SOLDIER IN THE FIRST SIKH WAR *by J W Baldwin*—Experiences of a private of H.M. 9th Regiment of Foot in the battles for the Punjab, India 1845-6.

TOMMY ATKINS' WAR STORIES: 14 FIRST HAND ACCOUNTS—Fourteen first hand accounts from the ranks of the British Army during Queen Victoria's Empire.

THE WATERLOO LETTERS *by H. T. Siborne*—Accounts of the Battle by British Officers for its Foremost Historian.

NEY: GENERAL OF CAVALRY VOLUME 1—1769-1799 *by Antoine Bulos*—The Early Career of a Marshal of the First Empire.

NEY: MARSHAL OF FRANCE VOLUME 2—1799-1805 *by Antoine Bulos*—The Early Career of a Marshal of the First Empire.

AIDE-DE-CAMP TO NAPOLEON *by Philippe-Paul de Ségur*—For anyone interested in the Napoleonic Wars this book, written by one who was intimate with the strategies and machinations of the Emperor, will be essential reading.

TWILIGHT OF EMPIRE *by Sir Thomas Ussher & Sir George Cockburn*—Two accounts of Napoleon's Journeys in Exile to Elba and St. Helena: Narrative of Events by Sir Thomas Ussher & Napoleon's Last Voyage: Extract of a diary by Sir George Cockburn.

PRIVATE WHEELER *by William Wheeler*—The letters of a soldier of the 51st Light Infantry during the Peninsular War & at Waterloo.

AVAILABLE ONLINE AT www.leonaur.com
AND FROM ALL GOOD BOOK STORES

07/09

LEONAUR

ALSO FROM LEONAUR
AVAILABLE IN SOFTCOVER OR HARDCOVER WITH DUST JACKET

OFFICERS & GENTLEMEN *by Peter Hawker & William Graham*—Two Accounts of British Officers During the Peninsula War: Officer of Light Dragoons by Peter Hawker & Campaign in Portugal and Spain by William Graham .

THE WALCHEREN EXPEDITION *by Anonymous*—The Experiences of a British Officer of the 81st Regt. During the Campaign in the Low Countries of 1809.

LADIES OF WATERLOO *by Charlotte A. Eaton, Magdalene de Lancey & Juana Smith*—The Experiences of Three Women During the Campaign of 1815: Waterloo Days by Charlotte A. Eaton, A Week at Waterloo by Magdalene de Lancey & Juana's Story by Juana Smith.

JOURNAL OF AN OFFICER IN THE KING'S GERMAN LEGION *by John Frederick Hering*—Recollections of Campaigning During the Napoleonic Wars.

JOURNAL OF AN ARMY SURGEON IN THE PENINSULAR WAR *by Charles Boutflower*—The Recollections of a British Army Medical Man on Campaign During the Napoleonic Wars.

ON CAMPAIGN WITH MOORE AND WELLINGTON *by Anthony Hamilton*—The Experiences of a Soldier of the 43rd Regiment During the Peninsular War.

THE ROAD TO AUSTERLITZ *by R. G. Burton*—Napoleon's Campaign of 1805.

SOLDIERS OF NAPOLEON *by A. J. Doisy De Villargennes & Arthur Chuquet*—The Experiences of the Men of the French First Empire: Under the Eagles by A. J. Doisy De Villargennes & Voices of 1812 by Arthur Chuquet .

INVASION OF FRANCE, 1814 *by F. W. O. Maycock*—The Final Battles of the Napoleonic First Empire.

LEIPZIG—A CONFLICT OF TITANS *by Frederic Shoberl*—A Personal Experience of the 'Battle of the Nations' During the Napoleonic Wars, October 14th-19th, 1813.

SLASHERS *by Charles Cadell*—The Campaigns of the 28th Regiment of Foot During the Napoleonic Wars by a Serving Officer.

BATTLE IMPERIAL *by Charles William Vane*—The Campaigns in Germany & France for the Defeat of Napoleon 1813-1814.

SWIFT & BOLD *by Gibbes Rigaud*—The 60th Rifles During the Peninsula War.

AVAILABLE ONLINE AT **www.leonaur.com**
AND FROM ALL GOOD BOOK STORES

07/09

LEONAUR

ALSO FROM LEONAUR
AVAILABLE IN SOFTCOVER OR HARDCOVER WITH DUST JACKET

ADVENTURES OF A YOUNG RIFLEMAN *by Johann Christian Maempel*—The Experiences of a Saxon in the French & British Armies During the Napoleonic Wars.

THE HUSSAR *by Norbert Landsheit & G. R. Gleig*—A German Cavalryman in British Service Throughout the Napoleonic Wars.

RECOLLECTIONS OF THE PENINSULA *by Moyle Sherer*—An Officer of the 34th Regiment of Foot—'The Cumberland Gentlemen'—on Campaign Against Napoleon's French Army in Spain.

MARINE OF REVOLUTION & CONSULATE *by Moreau de Jonnès*—The Recollections of a French Soldier of the Revolutionary Wars 1791-1804.

GENTLEMEN IN RED *by John Dobbs & Robert Knowles*—Two Accounts of British Infantry Officers During the Peninsular War Recollections of an Old 52nd Man by John Dobbs An Officer of Fusiliers by Robert Knowles.

CORPORAL BROWN'S CAMPAIGNS IN THE LOW COUNTRIES *by Robert Brown*—Recollections of a Coldstream Guard in the Early Campaigns Against Revolutionary France 1793-1795.

THE 7TH (QUEENS OWN) HUSSARS: Volume 2—1793-1815 *by C. R. B. Barrett*—During the Campaigns in the Low Countries & the Peninsula and Waterloo Campaigns of the Napoleonic Wars. Volume 2: 1793-1815.

THE MARENGO CAMPAIGN 1800 *by Herbert H. Sargent*—The Victory that Completed the Austrian Defeat in Italy.

DONALDSON OF THE 94TH—SCOTS BRIGADE *by Joseph Donaldson*—The Recollections of a Soldier During the Peninsula & South of France Campaigns of the Napoleonic Wars.

A CONSCRIPT FOR EMPIRE *by Philippe as told to Johann Christian Maempel*—The Experiences of a Young German Conscript During the Napoleonic Wars.

JOURNAL OF THE CAMPAIGN OF 1815 *by Alexander Cavalié Mercer*—The Experiences of an Officer of the Royal Horse Artillery During the Waterloo Campaign.

NAPOLEON'S CAMPAIGNS IN POLAND 1806-7 *by Robert Wilson*—The campaign in Poland from the Russian side of the conflict.

AVAILABLE ONLINE AT **www.leonaur.com**
AND FROM ALL GOOD BOOK STORES

07/09

LEONAUR

ALSO FROM LEONAUR

AVAILABLE IN SOFTCOVER OR HARDCOVER WITH DUST JACKET

OMPTEDA OF THE KING'S GERMAN LEGION *by Christian von Ompteda*—A Hanoverian Officer on Campaign Against Napoleon.

LIEUTENANT SIMMONS OF THE 95TH (RIFLES) *by George Simmons*—Recollections of the Peninsula, South of France & Waterloo Campaigns of the Napoleonic Wars.

A HORSEMAN FOR THE EMPEROR *by Jean Baptiste Gazzola*—A Cavalryman of Napoleon's Army on Campaign Throughout the Napoleonic Wars.

SERGEANT LAWRENCE *by William Lawrence*—With the 40th Regt. of Foot in South America, the Peninsular War & at Waterloo.

CAMPAIGNS WITH THE FIELD TRAIN *by Richard D. Henegan*—Experiences of a British Officer During the Peninsula and Waterloo Campaigns of the Napoleonic Wars.

CAVALRY SURGEON *by S. D. Broughton*—On Campaign Against Napoleon in the Peninsula & South of France During the Napoleonic Wars 1812-1814.

MEN OF THE RIFLES *by Thomas Knight, Henry Curling & Jonathan Leach*—The Reminiscences of Thomas Knight of the 95th (Rifles) by Thomas Knight, Henry Curling's Anecdotes by Henry Curling & The Field Services of the Rifle Brigade from its Formation to Waterloo by Jonathan Leach.

THE ULM CAMPAIGN 1805 *by F. N. Maude*—Napoleon and the Defeat of the Austrian Army During the 'War of the Third Coalition'.

SOLDIERING WITH THE 'DIVISION' *by Thomas Garrety*—The Military Experiences of an Infantryman of the 43rd Regiment During the Napoleonic Wars.

SERGEANT MORRIS OF THE 73RD FOOT *by Thomas Morris*—The Experiences of a British Infantryman During the Napoleonic Wars-Including Campaigns in Germany and at Waterloo.

A VOICE FROM WATERLOO *by Edward Cotton*—The Personal Experiences of a British Cavalryman Who Became a Battlefield Guide and Authority on the Campaign of 1815.

NAPOLEON AND HIS MARSHALS *by J. T. Headley*—The Men of the First Empire.

AVAILABLE ONLINE AT **www.leonaur.com**
AND FROM ALL GOOD BOOK STORES

07/09

LEONAUR

ALSO FROM LEONAUR
AVAILABLE IN SOFTCOVER OR HARDCOVER WITH DUST JACKET

COLBORNE: A SINGULAR TALENT FOR WAR *by John Colborne*—The Napoleonic Wars Career of One of Wellington's Most Highly Valued Officers in Egypt, Holland, Italy, the Peninsula and at Waterloo.

NAPOLEON'S RUSSIAN CAMPAIGN *by Philippe Henri de Segur*—The Invasion, Battles and Retreat by an Aide-de-Camp on the Emperor's Staff.

WITH THE LIGHT DIVISION *by John H. Cooke*—The Experiences of an Officer of the 43rd Light Infantry in the Peninsula and South of France During the Napoleonic Wars.

WELLINGTON AND THE PYRENEES CAMPAIGN VOLUME I: FROM VITORIA TO THE BIDASSOA *by F. C. Beatson*—The final phase of the campaign in the Iberian Peninsula.

WELLINGTON AND THE INVASION OF FRANCE VOLUME II: THE BIDASSOA TO THE BATTLE OF THE NIVELLE *by F. C. Beatson*—The final phase of the campaign in the Iberian Peninsula.

WELLINGTON AND THE FALL OF FRANCE VOLUME III: THE GAVES AND THE BATTLE OF ORTHEZ *by F. C. Beatson*—The final phase of the campaign in the Iberian Peninsula.

NAPOLEON'S IMPERIAL GUARD: FROM MARENGO TO WATERLOO *by J. T. Headley*—The story of Napoleon's Imperial Guard and the men who commanded them.

BATTLES & SIEGES OF THE PENINSULAR WAR *by W. H. Fitchett*—Corunna, Busaco, Albuera, Ciudad Rodrigo, Badajos, Salamanca, San Sebastian & Others.

SERGEANT GUILLEMARD: THE MAN WHO SHOT NELSON? *by Robert Guillemard*—A Soldier of the Infantry of the French Army of Napoleon on Campaign Throughout Europe.

WITH THE GUARDS ACROSS THE PYRENEES *by Robert Batty*—The Experiences of a British Officer of Wellington's Army During the Battles for the Fall of Napoleonic France, 1813 .

A STAFF OFFICER IN THE PENINSULA *by E. W. Buckham*—An Officer of the British Staff Corps Cavalry During the Peninsula Campaign of the Napoleonic Wars.

THE LEIPZIG CAMPAIGN: 1813—NAPOLEON AND THE "BATTLE OF THE NATIONS" *by F. N. Maude*—Colonel Maude's analysis of Napoleon's campaign of 1813 around Leipzig.

AVAILABLE ONLINE AT www.leonaur.com
AND FROM ALL GOOD BOOK STORES
07/09

LEONAUR

ALSO FROM LEONAUR
AVAILABLE IN SOFTCOVER OR HARDCOVER WITH DUST JACKET

BUGEAUD: A PACK WITH A BATON *by Thomas Robert Bugeaud*—The Early Campaigns of a Soldier of Napoleon's Army Who Would Become a Marshal of France.

WATERLOO RECOLLECTIONS *by Frederick Llewellyn*—Rare First Hand Accounts, Letters, Reports and Retellings from the Campaign of 1815.

SERGEANT NICOL *by Daniel Nicol*—The Experiences of a Gordon Highlander During the Napoleonic Wars in Egypt, the Peninsula and France.

THE JENA CAMPAIGN: 1806 *by F. N. Maude*—The Twin Battles of Jena & Auerstadt Between Napoleon's French and the Prussian Army.

PRIVATE O'NEIL *by Charles O'Neil*—The recollections of an Irish Rogue of H. M. 28th Regt.—The Slashers—during the Peninsula & Waterloo campaigns of the Napoleonic war.

ROYAL HIGHLANDER *by James Anton*—A soldier of H.M 42nd (Royal) Highlanders during the Peninsular, South of France & Waterloo Campaigns of the Napoleonic Wars.

CAPTAIN BLAZE *by Elzéar Blaze*—Life in Napoleons Army.

LEJEUNE VOLUME 1 *by Louis-François Lejeune*—The Napoleonic Wars through the Experiences of an Officer on Berthier's Staff.

LEJEUNE VOLUME 2 *by Louis-François Lejeune*—The Napoleonic Wars through the Experiences of an Officer on Berthier's Staff.

CAPTAIN COIGNET *by Jean-Roch Coignet*—A Soldier of Napoleon's Imperial Guard from the Italian Campaign to Russia and Waterloo.

FUSILIER COOPER *by John S. Cooper*—Experiences in the 7th (Royal) Fusiliers During the Peninsular Campaign of the Napoleonic Wars and the American Campaign to New Orleans.

FIGHTING NAPOLEON'S EMPIRE *by Joseph Anderson*—The Campaigns of a British Infantryman in Italy, Egypt, the Peninsular & the West Indies During the Napoleonic Wars.

CHASSEUR BARRES *by Jean-Baptiste Barres*—The experiences of a French Infantryman of the Imperial Guard at Austerlitz, Jena, Eylau, Friedland, in the Peninsular, Lutzen, Bautzen, Zinnwald and Hanau during the Napoleonic Wars.

AVAILABLE ONLINE AT www.leonaur.com
AND FROM ALL GOOD BOOK STORES

07/09

LEONAUR

ALSO FROM LEONAUR

AVAILABLE IN SOFTCOVER OR HARDCOVER WITH DUST JACKET

CAPTAIN COIGNET *by Jean-Roch Coignet*—A Soldier of Napoleon's Imperial Guard from the Italian Campaign to Russia and Waterloo.

HUSSAR ROCCA *by Albert Jean Michel de Rocca*—A French cavalry officer's experiences of the Napoleonic Wars and his views on the Peninsular Campaigns against the Spanish, British And Guerilla Armies.

MARINES TO 95TH (RIFLES) *by Thomas Fernyhough*—The military experiences of Robert Fernyhough during the Napoleonic Wars.

LIGHT BOB *by Robert Blakeney*—The experiences of a young officer in H.M 28th & 36th regiments of the British Infantry during the Peninsular Campaign of the Napoleonic Wars 1804 - 1814.

WITH WELLINGTON'S LIGHT CAVALRY *by William Tomkinson*—The Experiences of an officer of the 16th Light Dragoons in the Peninsular and Waterloo campaigns of the Napoleonic Wars.

SERGEANT BOURGOGNE *by Adrien Bourgogne*—With Napoleon's Imperial Guard in the Russian Campaign and on the Retreat from Moscow 1812 - 13.

SURTEES OF THE 95TH (RIFLES) *by William Surtees*—A Soldier of the 95th (Rifles) in the Peninsular campaign of the Napoleonic Wars.

SWORDS OF HONOUR *by Henry Newbolt & Stanley L. Wood*—The Careers of Six Outstanding Officers from the Napoleonic Wars, the Wars for India and the American Civil War.

ENSIGN BELL IN THE PENINSULAR WAR *by George Bell*—The Experiences of a young British Soldier of the 34th Regiment 'The Cumberland Gentlemen' in the Napoleonic wars.

HUSSAR IN WINTER *by Alexander Gordon*—A British Cavalry Officer during the retreat to Corunna in the Peninsular campaign of the Napoleonic Wars.

THE COMPLEAT RIFLEMAN HARRIS *by Benjamin Harris as told to and transcribed by Captain Henry Curling, 52nd Regt. of Foot*—The adventures of a soldier of the 95th (Rifles) during the Peninsular Campaign of the Napoleonic Wars.

THE ADVENTURES OF A LIGHT DRAGOON *by George Farmer & G.R. Gleig*—A cavalryman during the Peninsular & Waterloo Campaigns, in captivity & at the siege of Bhurtpore, India.

AVAILABLE ONLINE AT www.leonaur.com
AND FROM ALL GOOD BOOK STORES

07/09

LEONAUR

ALSO FROM LEONAUR
AVAILABLE IN SOFTCOVER OR HARDCOVER WITH DUST JACKET

THE LIFE OF THE REAL BRIGADIER GERARD VOLUME 1—THE YOUNG HUSSAR 1782-1807 *by Jean-Baptiste De Marbot*—A French Cavalryman Of the Napoleonic Wars at Marengo, Austerlitz, Jena, Eylau & Friedland.

THE LIFE OF THE REAL BRIGADIER GERARD VOLUME 2—IMPERIAL AIDE-DE-CAMP 1807-1811 *by Jean-Baptiste De Marbot*—A French Cavalryman of the Napoleonic Wars at Saragossa, Landshut, Eckmuhl, Ratisbon, Aspern-Essling, Wagram, Busaco & Torres Vedras.

THE LIFE OF THE REAL BRIGADIER GERARD VOLUME 3—COLONEL OF CHASSEURS 1811-1815 *by Jean-Baptiste De Marbot*—A French Cavalryman in the retreat from Moscow, Lutzen, Bautzen, Katzbach, Leipzig, Hanau & Waterloo.

THE INDIAN WAR OF 1864 *by Eugene Ware*—The Experiences of a Young Officer of the 7th Iowa Cavalry on the Western Frontier During the Civil War.

THE MARCH OF DESTINY *by Charles E. Young & V. Devinny*—Dangers of the Trail in 1865 by Charles E. Young & The Story of a Pioneer by V. Devinny, two Accounts of Early Emigrants to Colorado.

CROSSING THE PLAINS *by William Audley Maxwell*—A First Hand Narrative of the Early Pioneer Trail to California in 1857.

CHIEF OF SCOUTS *by William F. Drannan*—A Pilot to Emigrant and Government Trains, Across the Plains of the Western Frontier.

THIRTY-ONE YEARS ON THE PLAINS AND IN THE MOUNTAINS *by William F. Drannan*—William Drannan was born to be a pioneer, hunter, trapper and wagon train guide during the momentous days of the Great American West.

THE INDIAN WARS VOLUNTEER *by William Thompson*—Recollections of the Conflict Against the Snakes, Shoshone, Bannocks, Modocs and Other Native Tribes of the American North West.

THE 4TH TENNESSEE CAVALRY *by George B. Guild*—The Services of Smith's Regiment of Confederate Cavalry by One of its Officers.

COLONEL WORTHINGTON'S SHILOH *by T. Worthington*—The Tennessee Campaign, 1862, by an Officer of the Ohio Volunteers.

FOUR YEARS IN THE SADDLE *by W. L. Curry*—The History of the First Regiment Ohio Volunteer Cavalry in the American Civil War.

AVAILABLE ONLINE AT **www.leonaur.com**
AND FROM ALL GOOD BOOK STORES

07/09

ALSO FROM LEONAUR
AVAILABLE IN SOFTCOVER OR HARDCOVER WITH DUST JACKET

LIFE IN THE ARMY OF NORTHERN VIRGINIA *by Carlton McCarthy*— The Observations of a Confederate Artilleryman of Cutshaw's Battalion During the American Civil War 1861-1865.

HISTORY OF THE CAVALRY OF THE ARMY OF THE POTOMAC *by Charles D. Rhodes*—Including Pope's Army of Virginia and the Cavalry Operations in West Virginia During the American Civil War.

CAMP-FIRE AND COTTON-FIELD *by Thomas W. Knox*—A New York Herald Correspondent's View of the American Civil War.

SERGEANT STILLWELL *by Leander Stillwell*—The Experiences of a Union Army Soldier of the 61st Illinois Infantry During the American Civil War.

STONEWALL'S CANNONEER *by Edward A. Moore*—Experiences with the Rockbridge Artillery, Confederate Army of Northern Virginia, During the American Civil War.

THE SIXTH CORPS *by George Stevens*—The Army of the Potomac, Union Army, During the American Civil War.

THE RAILROAD RAIDERS *by William Pittenger*—An Ohio Volunteers Recollections of the Andrews Raid to Disrupt the Confederate Railroad in Georgia During the American Civil War.

CITIZEN SOLDIER *by John Beatty*—An Account of the American Civil War by a Union Infantry Officer of Ohio Volunteers Who Became a Brigadier General.

COX: PERSONAL RECOLLECTIONS OF THE CIVIL WAR--VOLUME 1 *by Jacob Dolson Cox*—West Virginia, Kanawha Valley, Gauley Bridge, Cotton Mountain, South Mountain, Antietam, the Morgan Raid & the East Tennessee Campaign.

COX: PERSONAL RECOLLECTIONS OF THE CIVIL WAR--VOLUME 2 *by Jacob Dolson Cox*—Siege of Knoxville, East Tennessee, Atlanta Campaign, the Nashville Campaign & the North Carolina Campaign.

KERSHAW'S BRIGADE VOLUME 1 *by D. Augustus Dickert*—Manassas, Seven Pines, Sharpsburg (Antietam), Fredricksburg, Chancellorsville, Gettysburg, Chickamauga, Chattanooga, Fort Sanders & Bean Station.

KERSHAW'S BRIGADE VOLUME 2 *by D. Augustus Dickert*—At the wilderness, Cold Harbour, Petersburg, The Shenandoah Valley and Cedar Creek..

AVAILABLE ONLINE AT www.leonaur.com
AND FROM ALL GOOD BOOK STORES
07/09

LEONAUR

ALSO FROM LEONAUR

AVAILABLE IN SOFTCOVER OR HARDCOVER WITH DUST JACKET

THE RELUCTANT REBEL *by William G. Stevenson*—A young Kentuckian's experiences in the Confederate Infantry & Cavalry during the American Civil War..

BOOTS AND SADDLES *by Elizabeth B. Custer*—The experiences of General Custer's Wife on the Western Plains.

FANNIE BEERS' CIVIL WAR *by Fannie A. Beers*—A Confederate Lady's Experiences of Nursing During the Campaigns & Battles of the American Civil War.

LADY SALE'S AFGHANISTAN *by Florentia Sale*—An Indomitable Victorian Lady's Account of the Retreat from Kabul During the First Afghan War.

THE TWO WARS OF MRS DUBERLY *by Frances Isabella Duberly*—An Intrepid Victorian Lady's Experience of the Crimea and Indian Mutiny.

THE REBELLIOUS DUCHESS *by Paul F. S. Dermoncourt*—The Adventures of the Duchess of Berri and Her Attempt to Overthrow French Monarchy.

LADIES OF WATERLOO *by Charlotte A. Eaton, Magdalene de Lancey & Juana Smith*—The Experiences of Three Women During the Campaign of 1815: Waterloo Days by Charlotte A. Eaton, A Week at Waterloo by Magdalene de Lancey & Juana's Story by Juana Smith.

TWO YEARS BEFORE THE MAST *by Richard Henry Dana. Jr.*—The account of one young man's experiences serving on board a sailing brig—the Penelope—bound for California, between the years 1834-36.

A SAILOR OF KING GEORGE *by Frederick Hoffman*—From Midshipman to Captain—Recollections of War at Sea in the Napoleonic Age 1793-1815.

LORDS OF THE SEA *by A. T. Mahan*—Great Captains of the Royal Navy During the Age of Sail.

COGGESHALL'S VOYAGES: VOLUME 1 *by George Coggeshall*—The Recollections of an American Schooner Captain.

COGGESHALL'S VOYAGES: VOLUME 2 *by George Coggeshall*—The Recollections of an American Schooner Captain.

TWILIGHT OF EMPIRE *by Sir Thomas Ussher & Sir George Cockburn*—Two accounts of Napoleon's Journeys in Exile to Elba and St. Helena: Narrative of Events by Sir Thomas Ussher & Napoleon's Last Voyage: Extract of a diary by Sir George Cockburn.

AVAILABLE ONLINE AT www.leonaur.com
AND FROM ALL GOOD BOOK STORES

07/09

LEONAUR

ALSO FROM LEONAUR
AVAILABLE IN SOFTCOVER OR HARDCOVER WITH DUST JACKET

ESCAPE FROM THE FRENCH *by Edward Boys*—A Young Royal Navy Midshipman's Adventures During the Napoleonic War.

THE VOYAGE OF H.M.S. PANDORA *by Edward Edwards R. N. & George Hamilton, edited by Basil Thomson*—In Pursuit of the Mutineers of the Bounty in the South Seas—1790-1791.

MEDUSA *by J. B. Henry Savigny and Alexander Correard and Charlotte-Adélaïde Dard* —Narrative of a Voyage to Senegal in 1816 & The Sufferings of the Picard Family After the Shipwreck of the Medusa.

THE SEA WAR OF 1812 VOLUME 1 *by A. T. Mahan*—A History of the Maritime Conflict.

THE SEA WAR OF 1812 VOLUME 2 *by A. T. Mahan*—A History of the Maritime Conflict.

WETHERELL OF H. M. S. HUSSAR *by John Wetherell*—The Recollections of an Ordinary Seaman of the Royal Navy During the Napoleonic Wars.

THE NAVAL BRIGADE IN NATAL *by C. R. N. Burne*—With the Guns of H. M. S. Terrible & H. M. S. Tartar during the Boer War 1899-1900.

THE VOYAGE OF H. M. S. BOUNTY *by William Bligh*—The True Story of an 18th Century Voyage of Exploration and Mutiny.

SHIPWRECK! *by William Gilly*—The Royal Navy's Disasters at Sea 1793-1849.

KING'S CUTTERS AND SMUGGLERS: 1700-1855 *by E. Keble Chatterton*—A unique period of maritime history-from the beginning of the eighteenth to the middle of the nineteenth century when British seamen risked all to smuggle valuable goods from wool to tea and spirits from and to the Continent.

CONFEDERATE BLOCKADE RUNNER *by John Wilkinson*—The Personal Recollections of an Officer of the Confederate Navy.

NAVAL BATTLES OF THE NAPOLEONIC WARS *by W. H. Fitchett*—Cape St. Vincent, the Nile, Cadiz, Copenhagen, Trafalgar & Others.

PRISONERS OF THE RED DESERT *by R. S. Gwatkin-Williams*—The Adventures of the Crew of the Tara During the First World War.

U-BOAT WAR 1914-1918 *by James B. Connolly/Karl von Schenk*—Two Contrasting Accounts from Both Sides of the Conflict at Sea D uring the Great War.

AVAILABLE ONLINE AT www.leonaur.com
AND FROM ALL GOOD BOOK STORES

07/09

ALSO FROM LEONAUR

AVAILABLE IN SOFTCOVER OR HARDCOVER WITH DUST JACKET

IRON TIMES WITH THE GUARDS *by An O. E. (G. P. A. Fildes)*—The Experiences of an Officer of the Coldstream Guards on the Western Front During the First World War.

THE GREAT WAR IN THE MIDDLE EAST: 1 *by W. T. Massey*—The Desert Campaigns & How Jerusalem Was Won---two classic accounts in one volume.

THE GREAT WAR IN THE MIDDLE EAST: 2 *by W. T. Massey*—Allenby's Final Triumph.

SMITH-DORRIEN *by Horace Smith-Dorrien*—Isandlwhana to the Great War.

1914 *by Sir John French*—The Early Campaigns of the Great War by the British Commander.

GRENADIER *by E. R. M. Fryer*—The Recollections of an Officer of the Grenadier Guards throughout the Great War on the Western Front.

BATTLE, CAPTURE & ESCAPE *by George Pearson*—The Experiences of a Canadian Light Infantryman During the Great War.

DIGGERS AT WAR *by R. Hugh Knyvett & G. P. Cuttriss*—"Over There" With the Australians by R. Hugh Knyvett and Over the Top With the Third Australian Division by G. P. Cuttriss. Accounts of Australians During the Great War in the Middle East, at Gallipoli and on the Western Front.

HEAVY FIGHTING BEFORE US *by George Brenton Laurie*—The Letters of an Officer of the Royal Irish Rifles on the Western Front During the Great War.

THE CAMELIERS *by Oliver Hogue*—A Classic Account of the Australians of the Imperial Camel Corps During the First World War in the Middle East.

RED DUST *by Donald Black*—A Classic Account of Australian Light Horsemen in Palestine During the First World War.

THE LEAN, BROWN MEN *by Angus Buchanan*—Experiences in East Africa During the Great War with the 25th Royal Fusiliers—the Legion of Frontiersmen.

THE NIGERIAN REGIMENT IN EAST AFRICA *by W. D. Downes*—On Campaign During the Great War 1916-1918.

THE 'DIE-HARDS' IN SIBERIA *by John Ward*—With the Middlesex Regiment Against the Bolsheviks 1918-19.

AVAILABLE ONLINE AT www.leonaur.com
AND FROM ALL GOOD BOOK STORES
07/09

LEONAUR

ALSO FROM LEONAUR

AVAILABLE IN SOFTCOVER OR HARDCOVER WITH DUST JACKET

FARAWAY CAMPAIGN *by F. James*—Experiences of an Indian Army Cavalry Officer in Persia & Russia During the Great War.

REVOLT IN THE DESERT *by T. E. Lawrence*—An account of the experiences of one remarkable British officer's war from his own perspective.

MACHINE-GUN SQUADRON *by A. M. G.*—The 20th Machine Gunners from British Yeomanry Regiments in the Middle East Campaign of the First World War.

A GUNNER'S CRUSADE *by Antony Bluett*—The Campaign in the Desert, Palestine & Syria as Experienced by the Honourable Artillery Company During the Great War .

DESPATCH RIDER *by W. H. L. Watson*—The Experiences of a British Army Motorcycle Despatch Rider During the Opening Battles of the Great War in Europe.

TIGERS ALONG THE TIGRIS *by E. J. Thompson*—The Leicestershire Regiment in Mesopotamia During the First World War.

HEARTS & DRAGONS *by Charles R. M. F. Crutwell*—The 4th Royal Berkshire Regiment in France and Italy During the Great War, 1914-1918.

INFANTRY BRIGADE: 1914 *by John Ward*—The Diary of a Commander of the 15th Infantry Brigade, 5th Division, British Army, During the Retreat from Mons.

DOING OUR 'BIT' *by Ian Hay*—Two Classic Accounts of the Men of Kitchener's 'New Army' During the Great War including *The First 100,000* & *All In It*.

AN EYE IN THE STORM *by Arthur Ruhl*—An American War Correspondent's Experiences of the First World War from the Western Front to Gallipoli-and Beyond.

STAND & FALL *by Joe Cassells*—With the Middlesex Regiment Against the Bolsheviks 1918-19.

RIFLEMAN MACGILL'S WAR *by Patrick MacGill*—A Soldier of the London Irish During the Great War in Europe including *The Amateur Army*, *The Red Horizon* & *The Great Push*.

WITH THE GUNS *by C. A. Rose & Hugh Dalton*—Two First Hand Accounts of British Gunners at War in Europe During World War 1- Three Years in France with the Guns and With the British Guns in Italy.

THE BUSH WAR DOCTOR *by Robert V. Dolbey*—The Experiences of a British Army Doctor During the East African Campaign of the First World War.

AVAILABLE ONLINE AT **www.leonaur.com**
AND FROM ALL GOOD BOOK STORES

07/09

LEONAUR

ALSO FROM LEONAUR
AVAILABLE IN SOFTCOVER OR HARDCOVER WITH DUST JACKET

THE 9TH—THE KING'S (LIVERPOOL REGIMENT) IN THE GREAT WAR 1914 - 1918 *by Enos H. G. Roberts*—Mersey to mud—war and Liverpool men.

THE GAMBARDIER *by Mark Severn*—The experiences of a battery of Heavy artillery on the Western Front during the First World War.

FROM MESSINES TO THIRD YPRES *by Thomas Floyd*—A personal account of the First World War on the Western front by a 2/5th Lancashire Fusilier.

THE IRISH GUARDS IN THE GREAT WAR - VOLUME 1 *by Rudyard Kipling*—Edited and Compiled from Their Diaries and Papers—The First Battalion.

THE IRISH GUARDS IN THE GREAT WAR - VOLUME 1 *by Rudyard Kipling*—Edited and Compiled from Their Diaries and Papers—The Second Battalion.

ARMOURED CARS IN EDEN *by K. Roosevelt*—An American President's son serving in Rolls Royce armoured cars with the British in Mesopatamia & with the American Artillery in France during the First World War.

CHASSEUR OF 1914 *by Marcel Dupont*—Experiences of the twilight of the French Light Cavalry by a young officer during the early battles of the great war in Europe.

TROOP HORSE & TRENCH *by R.A. Lloyd*—The experiences of a British Lifeguardsman of the household cavalry fighting on the western front during the First World War 1914-18.

THE EAST AFRICAN MOUNTED RIFLES *by C.J. Wilson*—Experiences of the campaign in the East African bush during the First World War.

THE LONG PATROL *by George Berrie*—A Novel of Light Horsemen from Gallipoli to the Palestine campaign of the First World War.

THE FIGHTING CAMELIERS *by Frank Reid*—The exploits of the Imperial Camel Corps in the desert and Palestine campaigns of the First World War.

STEEL CHARIOTS IN THE DESERT *by S. C. Rolls*—The first world war experiences of a Rolls Royce armoured car driver with the Duke of Westminster in Libya and in Arabia with T.E. Lawrence.

WITH THE IMPERIAL CAMEL CORPS IN THE GREAT WAR *by Geoffrey Inchbald*—The story of a serving officer with the British 2nd battalion against the Senussi and during the Palestine campaign.

AVAILABLE ONLINE AT **www.leonaur.com**
AND FROM ALL GOOD BOOK STORES
07/09

www.ingramcontent.com/pod-product-compliance
Lightning Source LLC
Chambersburg PA
CBHW032053080426
42733CB00006B/256

* 9 7 8 0 8 5 7 0 6 6 2 4 4 *